rooted

rooted

REDISCOVER THE JESSE TREE THIS ADVENT

Augustine Institute
Florissant, Missouri

Augustine Institute
16805 New Halls Ferry Road
Florissant, MO 63034
www.augustineinstitute.org

Cover Design: Bence Szasz
Writer: Dr. Scott Hefelfinger
Design Team: Ben Dybas, Madelynn Felix, Amy Frazier

ISBN: 978-1-955305-95-2
Ebook ISBN: 978-1-955305-96-9

Library of Congress Control Number 2024945765

Printed in Canada

Contents

Introduction

Happy Advent!

In my household, we love the season of Advent. It's such a joyful time of anticipation, for adults and children alike, as we look forward to Christ's coming at Christmas. But especially for adults, entering into that anticipation can be a challenge. So, this little book is designed to help overcome that challenge. Let me explain how.

Because we're often pressed for time as Christmas approaches, each chapter is designed to be short enough to fit into our full days but meaty enough to enrich our prayer and our lives. For brevity and substance, the popular devotion known as the Jesse Tree is perfect.

What is the Jesse Tree? Well, you're gonna find out! But let me say in advance that it is basically a devotion that highlights the major figures and events in Scripture leading up to the coming of Christ at Christmas. Ornaments for each biblical scene are often hung on a tree of some sort—which works really well for families—but it can also be done without. Although typically geared toward children, the Jesse Tree devotion is presented here in a way that is relevant and fruitful for adults.

A big part of this involves learning how to find our roots in Scripture and how these deep roots can bear rich fruit in our ordinary lives. Here, the *Catechism of the Catholic Church* is helpful for ensuring that we read the Bible with the mind of the Church. Scripture and the *Catechism* each shed light on the other and, taken together, they provide light, consolation, and challenge in our lives of discipleship. For this reason, nearly every meditation includes a reference to the *Catechism*.

In short, this book is meant to help enhance your prayer time during Advent in a profound way. It reinterprets the traditional devotion of the Jesse Tree for adults while also equipping you to share your insights with others around you or in your care.

How to Use This Book

Since this book is meant to deepen your prayer, it is meant to be read during, or in close connection with, time set aside for prayer, whether by yourself or with a group. Designed for this setting, each of the upcoming days offers a brief scriptural meditation and provides guidance for these to bear rich fruit in your life and in the lives of those around you.

First, a *scriptural passage* captures an important moment in the story of salvation. It goes without saying that the most important part of this book is the biblical part, which has been carefully selected to highlight the shape of salvation history and to make it understandable and familiar. So, these passages are to be read slowly, lovingly, prayerfully.

Next, a *meditation* helps you go beyond being acquainted with the biblical text to being intimately familiar with it. This means learning to see the biblical story with new eyes and then discovering how it applies to daily life.

After reading the meditation, the ideal path is to begin a conversation with God. What struck you about the scriptural passage, the meditation, or both? What is God trying to say to you through today's reflection? To help foster this conversation with God or start a discussion with others, some *questions for reflection or discussion* follow the meditation.

After spending time in reflection and conversation with God, each day puts forward some *resolutions to consider*. What is a resolution? Simply put, a resolution is a commitment, often quite small, made during prayer that extends or applies the time spent in prayer to the rest of the day, or to the next day if you're praying in the evening. Often, a resolution will look like applying a lesson learned or an insight gained during prayer. It might be very closely connected to the reading or meditation for the day, or it might be something else the Lord puts on your heart. Either way, the resolution is critical and, for this reason, this book offers a few resolutions as ideas or templates to consider implementing in your own life.

The last section of each day aims to equip you with a simple method to bring the Jesse Tree devotion to your family and to *build an Advent tradition* together. Of course, by extension, this section can also be used as a simple format for sharing the Jesse Tree devotion with others as well.

In a certain sense, it provides the shortest and simplest summary of each day so that you can be prepared to lead a little group prayer or conversation based on the Jesse Tree devotion for that day.

Each day you're prompted to "Put up your Jesse Tree ornament." What your ornament looks like and where you hang it is entirely up to you. We've suggested images so you can make your own, or ready-made ornaments can be bought (although they might not match all the stories presented in this book). Your "tree" can be as creative as you like: some twigs in a vase, your Christmas tree, or a family tree-like background on the wall. There are plenty of ideas online.

A final note: the Advent season can last anywhere from 22 to 28 days. This book offers 25 reflection days, making it easily adaptable to the length of any Advent season. If Advent is 22 days long, then three reflections are extra and can be either included by doubling up on three days, say Sundays, or saved for another year. (For the most balanced view of the scriptural story, I recommend treating days 17, 19, and 23 as extra.) If Advent is 28 days long, then three days can go without a reflection. One easy way of doing this would be to begin the Advent season with the Jesse Tree devotion on the first Sunday of Advent and then omit it on the remaining Sundays. There is a great deal of flexibility here, so however long Advent is, you should be able to adjust the number of reflections without too much effort.

Advent is a time to experience anew the sense of expectation and wonder that leads up to the coming of our Savior, Jesus Christ. It is my hope and prayer that this small book will enrich this liturgical season, helping this Advent to be especially fruitful for you and your loved ones.

Day 1

Creation and the Jesse Tree

The Story of Salvation: Genesis 1:1–13

In the beginning, God created the heavens and the earth. The earth was without form and void, and darkness was over the face of the deep; and the Spirit of God was moving over the face of the waters.

And God said, "Let there be light"; and there was light. And God saw that the light was good; and God separated the light from the darkness. God called the light Day, and the darkness he called Night. And there was evening and there was morning, one day.

And God said, "Let there be a firmament in the midst of the waters, and let it separate the waters from the waters." And God made the firmament and separated the waters which were under the firmament from the waters which were above the firmament. And it was so. And God called the firmament Heaven. And there was evening and there was morning, a second day.

And God said, "Let the waters under the heavens be gathered together into one place, and let the dry land appear." And it was so. God called the dry land Earth, and the waters that were gathered together he called Seas. And God saw that it was good. And God said, "Let the earth put forth vegetation, plants yielding seed, and fruit trees bearing fruit in which is their seed, each according to its kind, upon the earth." And it was so. The earth brought forth vegetation, plants yielding seed according to their own kinds, and trees bearing fruit in which is their seed, each according to its kind. And God saw that it was good. And there was evening and there was morning, a third day.

A Meditation for Today

Since we're at the beginning, we should start by answering the question: What is the Jesse Tree? A simple question, but it actually can be answered in different ways. So, we'll return to this question more than once as we continue through Advent, and each time we do, we'll understand it better. For now, let's begin with a pretty simple, practical answer: the Jesse Tree is an Advent tradition that walks us through the major figures and events of salvation history. It gives us a chance to reflect on the waiting of God's Chosen People before the coming of the Messiah. It helps us to appreciate how every moment in the story of salvation points to Christ's coming. Usually, it involves reading Scripture, praying, and decorating a tree with ornaments that depict these same scriptural moments. And that tree, with the ornaments, is called the Jesse Tree.

Okay, that's a good start at answering our question. But here's another one: We just read about creation, but how does it fit into Advent?

If Advent is meant to set the stage for Christmas, creation *is* the stage. We often take the stage for granted—but actually, the stage is a well-thought-out feat of engineering. At the most basic level, it raises up the setting and the actors so that the audience can see. At its most sophisticated level, it can have all sorts of moving parts and functions that all serve the drama being performed for an audience. The stage is never the focal point, but we shouldn't take it for granted.

Creation is similar. Scripture presents to us a remarkable and fascinating story: a drama, if you will. And so, looking for the performers and plot line, we can overlook the basic setting: creation. The book of Genesis certainly has remarkable characters and a gripping plot, but it opens by describing in detail the stage, the created world.

The first chapter of Genesis portrays the world as the result of divine wisdom and love. It's a place of goodness, order, and harmony. The language is at turns majestic and familiar. There are words and patterns in the text that highlight these very characteristics: God created, it was so, God looked, it was good, the first day, the second, the third.

This depiction is totally different from other creation accounts that were circulating at the time—and we can be grateful for that! Instead of a threatening world of competing divinities, violence, evil, and bloodshed, Genesis presents creation as a place of order, beauty, support, and, ultimately, love. The world is our stage ... and so much more!

It's a *garden*, providing for us in so many ways, from food to raw materials. It's our *home*, giving us shelter and supporting us as we live, grow, create culture, and love. But above all, it's a *temple*, a place where we are meant to encounter the Lord and enter into loving communion with him.

I don't think we usually think of creation in this way, but it's kind of the main point. The *Catechism of the Catholic Church* highlights this dimension in covenantal terms: "The revelation of creation is inseparable from the revelation and forging of the covenant of the one God with his People. Creation is revealed as the first step toward this covenant, the first and universal witness to God's all-powerful love" (288).

God's love draws us toward him. This same love drew his people toward him and into a covenant with him in the Old Testament. The first creation account accentuates this by having God speak ten times in creating the world. These "ten words" point ahead to the Ten Commandments, which are sometimes called the Decalogue ("ten words") and were given as part of the covenant established through Moses. So, creation is presented as the first step toward the covenant between God and his people. It provides the place where a people can live, come to know God, and enter into a covenant with him.

And the same is true today: creation is meant to be the place where we encounter God and enter into loving communion with him.

God is present in this temple, the temple of creation, in multiple ways, but the most dramatic was when God became man and lived among us. He entered into the temple that he himself created and he did this so that we would be able to meet him there, to witness his love, and to receive that love as our own through faith.

It's that dramatic moment, the Incarnation, that we're waiting for in Advent. And it's that crucial moment that all the stories of the Jesse Tree lead to. So, as we wait, we should remember that God lovingly prepared the world for his own entrance at Christmas. This preparation began by creating the world, by setting up the stage, and by building the temple where we can encounter him and enter into communion with him. So, let's not overlook the stage; let's not take creation for granted.

Questions for Reflection and Discussion

- Do you have a love affair with the natural world? Or is it more of a love-hate relationship? Or maybe it's just functional? How can remembering that God created the world change your perspective?

- To be led by creation back to God, we have to look beyond the immediate satisfaction that creation can provide us. This requires us to have the virtue of temperance, or moderation. How will we see God more clearly and appreciate the gift of creation if we have the virtue of temperance?

- Although modern science is often (wrongly) thought to be opposed to faith, how can its discoveries actually lead us to appreciate God's artistry in creation even more?

Resolutions to Consider

- Begin to cultivate a habit of seeing the world around you as God's loving gift by committing to giving thanks at one or two moments a day for the beauty and goodness of creation.

- Set aside time to pray while walking outdoors.

- Spend some moments reflecting on how God has given us a beautiful world as a place to meet with us, especially by sending his Son and drawing near to us in prayer.

Build a Family Tradition

- With your family, read or tell in your own words the creation account in Genesis 1.

- Appreciate the remarkable language and imagery in the creation story together. Note the main point: God created everything that exists, and he did so in a way that was well ordered, completely free, and full of love.

- Hang up your Jesse Tree ornament. (Suggested image: planet Earth)

- Discuss the following: *Creation is a work of art and God is the artist. What can we learn about God, the artist, by looking at creation, his artwork?*

Day 2

The Image of God

The Story of Salvation: Genesis 1:26–31

Then God said, "Let us make man in our image, after our like-ness; and let them have dominion over the fish of the sea, and over the birds of the air, and over the cattle, and over all the earth, and over every creeping thing that creeps upon the earth." So God created man in his own image, in the image of God he created him; male and female he created them. And God blessed them, and God said to them, "Be fruitful and multiply, and fill the earth and subdue it; and have dominion over the fish of the sea and over the birds of the air and over every living thing that moves upon the earth." And God said, "Behold, I have given you every plant yielding seed which is upon the face of all the earth, and every tree with seed in its fruit; you shall have them for food. And to every beast of the earth, and to every bird of the air, and to everything that creeps on the earth, everything that has the breath of life, I have given every green plant for food." And it was so. And God saw everything that he had made, and behold, it was very good. And there was evening and there was morning, a sixth day.

A Meditation for Today

The book of Genesis is certainly ancient, but it isn't irrelevant to us today. It's full of wisdom for us, and we see that here in the creation of man and woman. Just a few short verses give us a teaching of remarkable depth and relevance. But to see this we have to read closely and keep in mind the way the text builds to this moment. Some of the main features of Genesis chapter 1 are patterns that repeat: for example, God speaking, things being called good, days being numbered. So, if anything changes in the pattern, we should assume the author does this intentionally and with some meaning in mind.

Well, there *are* a few notable changes when we get to the final day of creation. Let me briefly highlight two of them.

First, man is said to be created in the image of God. This is an entirely new description we haven't seen before in the text. What does it mean? We usually think of it as telling us something about ourselves, and it does. But notice *how* it does that: it directs our attention to God. What is God like? Well, we look to the verses before this point, and we find that God creates (1) with great order, (2) with great care, making things to be and providing for their ongoing existence, and (3) without compulsion. In other words, God is intelligent, loving, and free. And so, if humans are made in the *image of* God, these same characteristics reflect what is special about humans: we can understand, we can love, and we have freedom.

So, why do we have these special abilities? To answer that, we have to look at the second change in the text's patterns: after the creation of man and woman, God doesn't call them good.

Wait, what?!

I know what you're thinking: we just read that humans are "very good." But did we really? Are we *really* paying attention to the text? It says, "God saw *everything* that he had made, and behold, it was very good" (Gen 1:31). Why doesn't God call human beings specifically good? It isn't because we're bad. But the sense that "good" has in Genesis here has to do with being complete, perfect. After the creation of human beings, the whole of creation is complete. But human beings are not perfect—we have to grow into our perfection, through physical growth but also and even more so through moral growth. Unlike the entire rest of visible creation, we are free. We have the freedom to turn toward evil or toward good, and only the latter leads to our perfection. In this way, we're incomplete at creation—not bad or evil, but good and on the way, hopefully, toward goodness, our perfection.

So, as human beings, we have a special standing in creation that gives rise to a special calling and responsibility: we are created in the image of God, and because of that, we're on the way toward perfection or completeness. There's something indeterminate about human beings because we're free. And with every free choice we make, our character becomes more and more determinate—like an artist's chisel that unearths from the stone a beautiful form with each precise blow of the hammer.

By presenting the gift and responsibility of our special standing, Genesis challenges what I think is a pretty common view: humans are basically good, most people are pretty friendly, and folks are generally "nice"—a word we often use—with some very few being either terribly bad or remarkably good. And against this view, Genesis insists that we are indeed good, but good *and on the way*; we are indeed free, but free *for the good*. We do have a special standing, but it's one that enables and requires us to work at each moment to achieve the fullness of what it means to be created in the image of God.

If that seems like a reality check, there's more where that came from. If we take into account our fallen human nature, the situation is even more precarious: because of the effects of Original Sin, we gravitate toward what is bad rather than what is good.

So, that's our healthy dose of realism for today—but it is not a cause for despair! It's Advent, and these are still early days. The one we are awaiting is the one who makes it possible to reflect on God more and more. None of us are "basically good" and fixed in that state. But that's because each and every one of us is called to greatness in and through Christ. As we await his coming, we should ask ourselves: in what areas of life do I think of myself as "basically good"? Where have I gotten comfortable with the status quo in imitating Christ? When we answer these questions honestly, we will find that our longing for Christ's coming only increases as we look for his help to grow into the goodness, the greatness, that we were created and redeemed for.

Questions for Reflection and Discussion

- Are you tempted to think of yourself as basically pretty good? Even if your external behavior is decent, what selfish motivations and weaknesses might lie beneath the surface?

- Self-knowledge is one key to growing in holiness. Saint Catherine of Siena reminds us that this means knowing both our sinfulness and God's enduring love for us. Are you tempted to feel like you're doing pretty well? Remember that God's love wants more of you. Are you tempted to feel like you're making no progress? Remember that God's love is always gently pushing you forward.

Resolutions to Consider

- Start forming a habit of examining your conscience at least once a day. Take a few minutes to thank God for the blessings and successes of the day and then to scrutinize your actions and motivations during the day. As you notice patterns, ask the Lord to help you to overcome these weaknesses.

- Commit to speaking a kind word to someone close to you, encouraging that person in his or her growth in goodness.

- Find one area in your life where some fear or attachment compromises the freedom that Christ wants you to have. Ask the Lord to help you to overcome this obstacle.

Build a Family Tradition

- With your family, read or tell in your own words the creation of man and woman in Genesis 1.

- Consider how special it is that we are created in God's image, made to know the truth and to give and receive love.

- Hang up your Jesse Tree ornament. (Suggested image: Adam and Eve)

- Discuss the following: *If we are created to know and to love, then doing these things makes us truly happy. What are some moments in life when we've experienced this happiness (maybe in knowing and loving a friend, God, or a special hobby or pursuit)?*

Day 3

The Great Refusal

The Story of Salvation: Genesis 3:1–8

Now the serpent was more subtle than any other wild creature that the LORD God had made. He said to the woman, "Did God say, 'You shall not eat of any tree of the garden'?" And the woman said to the serpent, "We may eat of the fruit of the trees of the garden; but God said, 'You shall not eat of the fruit of the tree which is in the midst of the garden, neither shall you touch it, lest you die.'" But the serpent said to the woman, "You will not die. For God knows that when you eat of it your eyes will be opened, and you will be like God, knowing good and evil." So when the woman saw that the tree was good for food, and that it was a delight to the eyes, and that the tree was to be desired to make one wise, she took of its fruit and ate; and she also gave some to her husband, and he ate. Then the eyes of both were opened, and they knew that they were naked; and they sewed fig leaves together and made themselves aprons.

And they heard the sound of the LORD God walking in the garden in the cool of the day, and the man and his wife hid themselves from the presence of the LORD God among the trees of the garden.

A Meditation for Today

Being independent doesn't seem like such a bad thing. After all, aren't we meant to take care of ourselves, to strive to be self-reliant, resourceful, and the like?

Yes, we are ... but it's a fine line. Being human involves providing for ourselves through our actions. That's part of what it means to be created in the image of God. God has providence over creation, and we image that providence in our own lives. In this sense, we are like God; we are made in his image. And yet, we are not entirely like God, and this is the threshold that the devil's temptation crosses: "When you eat the fruit of *that* tree, when you take the one fruit that is forbidden, when *you* make the rules of the game and set yourself up as completely independent of God's law—then you will be like God."

But how can we be like God when we go against him? How can we image or reflect God when we contravene what he says? How can we be provident like God when we go against what his providence has ordained?

We can't, and this is the line we must not cross: we can and should pursue a certain kind of independence and self-reliance, but not at the expense of depending on God and relying on his guidance, his laws. The *Catechism* puts it this way: "The 'tree of the knowledge of good and evil' symbolically evokes the insurmountable limits that man, being a creature, must freely recognize and respect with trust. Man is dependent on his Creator and subject to the laws of creation and to the moral norms that govern the use of freedom" (396).

Adam and Eve's original sin is mysterious. But at its heart, it is a great refusal. We usually think of them as *taking* something: fruit from a tree. And they do. But they grasp after something not given to them because they are unwilling to *receive* what has been given to them, the gift of a limit, a boundary, a law that is meant to ensure their flourishing. And so the underlying reality here is something much deeper and much more tragic than picking and eating a fruit. It is "the great refusal"—of dependence, of trust, of love, of who God is and of who they are as created in his image.

We constantly face the same temptation that Adam and Eve faced. We're tempted to grasp after things rather than to receive what is given. We're tempted to focus on ourselves rather than to attend to others. Think about it: are there gifts that God gives that you find yourself tempted to refuse? The gift of a challenge? The gift of a law or limit? The gift of his love, which cannot be earned, and yet we try to earn it and thus refuse it precisely as a gift? C. S. Lewis, in his book *Perelandra*, has a wise character who talks about accepting the given fruit—whatever that fruit may be: a given moment, a challenge, a person, a rule or law, a gift we may not have expected or perhaps may not have wanted.

Especially when it comes to the gift of God's law, we rationalize the things we do that we know are wrong. We tell ourselves, "They're not *so* wrong, and they'll bring about *some* good, and, after all, who can make the effort to listen to *every* word, follow *all* the rules, *to* the letter, *all* the time?"

You know who can? Someone who's in love. When the lover is in the presence of his beloved, he hangs on every word; he doesn't wait for a rule or even a request but instead seeks to please and to fulfill eagerly and in anticipation; and if a rule or request is forthcoming, fulfilling it feels easy, even if it's hard, and it brings with it delight ... and gratitude. Love makes obedience sweet and grateful.

Christ shows us this perfectly by taking on the greatest sacrifice out of love for us. And the beginning of that mystery is what we await in Advent.

When we think about our temptations to be independent and in control, to rely on ourselves and our wants even to the point of pretending to be independent of God and his divine guidance, we ought to keep in mind the best solution: love. The love that Christ models for us and then puts into our hearts through baptism and faith. Advent is a time of waiting, and as we wait, let's remember that we are waiting for the arrival of our beloved. And as love is enkindled and grows to burn brightly in our hearts, we'll find that what we were once tempted to refuse we now desire to accept—accepting our dependence on God becomes easy, and loving his law becomes sweet.

Questions for Reflection and Discussion

- When you think about being independent, how does it make you feel—exhilarated, strong, lonely, afraid? How can you acknowledge and deepen your dependence on God?

- Discerning the ways that we refuse God can be subtle. Sometimes we even do so with righteous motives: "I have to pray now; I don't have time to help my child/sibling/spouse." Where and when are you most tempted to refuse God in a subtle, crafty way?

Resolutions to Consider

- Spend a few moments today meditating on the Ten Commandments. Consider how these rules are a gift and an expression of God's love and guidance.

- Identify one major challenge in your life right now. How does it make you feel? Frustrated? Angry? Sad? Rebellious? Consider that God has given you this challenge because he loves you— how might that change your perspective?

- Go to confession or make a concrete plan to go this week. When you prepare for confession, ask yourself when you have refused God in some way—his love, a challenge, an invitation, someone in need, etc.

Build a Family Tradition

- With your family, read or tell in your own words the story of the fall in Genesis 3.

- Acknowledge how mysterious the story is and how that fits with how mysterious evil and sin are. Note the key point: Adam and Eve didn't trust God's command; they went against it by taking what wasn't given to them.

- Hang up your Jesse Tree ornament. (Suggested image: an apple)

- Discuss the following: *How might God have felt when Adam and Eve turned away from him? Why would he feel this way? Is it similar when we disobey him today?*

Day 4

Cain and His Descendants

The Story of Salvation: Genesis 4:9–17, 19–22

*Then the L*ORD *said to Cain, "Where is Abel your brother?" He said, "I do not know; am I my brother's keeper?" And the L*ORD *said, "What have you done? The voice of your brother's blood is crying to me from the ground. And now you are cursed from the ground ... When you till the ground, it shall no longer yield to you its strength; you shall be a fugitive and a wanderer on the earth." Cain said to the L*ORD, *"My punishment is greater than I can bear. Behold, you have driven me this day away from the ground; and from your face I shall be hidden; and I shall be a fugitive and a wanderer on the earth, and whoever finds me will slay me." Then the L*ORD *said to him, "Not so! If anyone slays Cain, vengeance shall be taken on him sevenfold." And the L*ORD *put a mark on Cain, lest any who came upon him should kill* *him. Then Cain went away from the presence of the LORD and dwelt in the land of Nod, east of Eden.*

Cain knew his wife, and she conceived and bore Enoch; and he built a city, and called the name of the city after the name of his son, Enoch. . . . La'mech took two wives; the name of the one was A'dah, and the name of the other Zillah. Adah bore Ja'bal; he was the father of those who dwell in tents and have cattle. His brother's name was Ju'bal; he was the father of all those who play the lyre and pipe. Zillah bore Tu'bal-cain; he was the forger of all instruments of bronze and iron.

A Meditation for Today

Cain is a living contradiction. He *relies on God* for his life, but then he also tries to *deny this reliance*. He takes matters into his own hands, most infamously taking his own brother's life in a misguided attempt to have his sacrifice approved as Abel's was.

I think if we're honest, we all often want to be in control. We're bombarded with messages telling us to be strong, self-sufficient, a "self-made man" or woman. And we have all sorts of tools to help! Productivity apps, gadgets galore, online resources, self-help books, health regimens, and on and on. Sure, we say we want to serve God and rely on him, but do we really mean it? Often, we say one thing, but our actions speak more loudly.

In other words, there is a little bit of Cain in each of us. Or, to put it otherwise, all of us are descendants of Cain. The *Catechism* reminds us of this when it talks about avarice or greed. We tend to think that these have to do with money, and they do. But even more than that, they have to do with power: "The tenth commandment forbids . . . avarice arising from a passion for riches and their attendant power" (2536). Riches have little use apart from what they enable us to buy or do, so power is what really underlies the unbridled pursuit of wealth. The desire for power is a deep-seated one, and this is one reason why greed is one of the seven capital vices.

The capital vices are not the worst possible sins, though we sometimes call them "the seven deadly sins." What makes them deadly is that they are the root sins, the sources from which many other sins spring forth. Most of the sins we commit can be traced back to the seven capital vices. So, avarice and its pursuit of power run deep indeed. And our desire for control shows that Cain lives on inside each of us.

How do we leave behind our inner Cain?

If we go back to Cain, we should notice that his punishment—to be "a fugitive and a wanderer on the earth" (Gen 4:12)—is actually a mercy. By wandering, Cain is meant to learn to rely on God rather than on his own skills as a settled, stable farmer. But what does Cain do? Scripture tells us he "settled in the land of Nod" (Gen 4:16)—he settled down again! Cain doesn't trust God. He continues to live a contradiction. "Nod" means wandering; it is the land of wanderers. But Cain doesn't wander; he settles. Not only that, but he also builds a city. Even more than a farm, a city is built for self-sufficiency. In a final nod to relying on man's own resources, Cain's descendants discover the arts and crafts:

tent makers for shelter, cattle ranchers for food, musicians for leisure, and metalworkers for tools.

Cain and his descendants are creative and resourceful, and these attributes manifest the ingenuity of human beings created in the image of God. But there's a caveat: being an image means we are not the source and, even more, it means we must rely upon the source. Without the source, the image ceases to exist.

When we reflect on our own gifts, talents, tools, and resources, we should ask ourselves—do these always serve our reliance on God, or do they undermine it? In the end, we begin to find the solution when we see that Cain is an *anti-type* of Christ; he points ahead to Christ by way of contrast. Cain takes matters into his own hands, but Christ always seeks to do his Father's will. Abel is the opposite of Cain; he offered a pleasing sacrifice to God, as Christ also did. This makes him a *type* of Christ: a precursor and anticipatory sign of Jesus Christ.

In Advent, we await the coming of Christ. While we wait, we remember those great figures who foreshadowed and prepared the way for Christ. Abel stands among these figures. As a type of Christ, his brief life reminds us of Christ's simple obedience to his Father's will and the pleasing sacrifice he made on the cross. But Cain, as an anti-type, can also help us prepare for Christ's coming. His murderous envy and his rejection of relying on God remind us of the evil that Christ came to triumph over and save us from. There is a little bit of Cain in each of us, and Advent is a time to leave behind our inner Cain and rediscover our inner Abel. It is a time to return to Christ and to prepare ourselves to rejoice ever more greatly at his coming.

Questions for Reflection and Discussion

- What are some of your gifts, talents, or resources? How do you use these to serve God and others? How can these tempt you to forget about God and to avoid relying on him?

- Human ingenuity is a marvelous thing. But Scripture traces human craft and skill back to the line of Cain. What can this teach us about the limits and temptations of art, culture, and technology?

- Think about how relying on God requires the virtues. For example, it takes hope and fortitude to trust and to rely on God; it takes temperance to use the products of art and technology in a way that doesn't try to control everything. What virtues do you need most right now?

Resolutions to Consider

- Reserve some time today, and every day, to be free from relying on technology and media.

- Remind yourself at least three times today that God is in control and that everything is a matter of his providence.

- Find one way to use your strength and resourcefulness to serve someone else's will or needs instead of your own.

Build a Family Tradition

- With your family, read or recall in your own words the story of Cain and Abel in Genesis 4.

- Help everyone to understand the weight of the tragedy. Note the main point: sin doesn't stop with Adam and Eve, but only gets worse, as we see in the life of Cain. (Suggested image: a sword)

- After putting up your Jesse Tree ornament, talk together about the question: *What are some ways that we like to be in control, and which of these could we give up or work on this Advent?*

Day 5

God Favors the Simple

The Story of Salvation: Genesis 6:4–6, 8–9, 13, 17–22

The Neph'ilim were on the earth in those days ... These were the mighty men that were of old, the men of renown.

The LORD saw that the wickedness of man was great in the earth, and that every imagination of the thoughts of his heart was only evil continually. And the LORD was sorry that he made man on the earth, and it grieved him to his heart. ... But Noah found favor in the eyes of the LORD.

... Noah was a righteous man, blameless in his generation; Noah walked with God.

God said to Noah, "I have determined to make an end of all flesh; for the earth is filled with violence through them; ... For behold, I will bring a flood of waters upon the earth, to destroy all flesh ... ; everything that is on the earth shall die. But I will establish my covenant with you; and you shall come into the ark, you, your sons, your wife, and your sons' wives with you. And of every living thing of all flesh, you shall bring two of every sort into the ark, to keep them alive with you; they shall be male and female. Of the birds according to their kinds, and of the animals according to their kinds, of every creeping thing of the ground according to its kind, two of every sort shall come in to you, to keep them alive. Also take with you every sort of food that is eaten, and store it up; and it shall serve as food for you and for them." Noah did this; he did all that God commanded him.

A Meditation for Today

After an epic opening about the Nephilim, the mighty men of the earth, the men of renown, Genesis 6 sort of just moves right along to the wickedness on the earth and then to Noah. It's almost a letdown. Where are the herculean exploits? Where are the heroic deeds?

This unexpected move makes a powerful point: God's favor takes no notice of the mighty men of the earth and instead rests upon Noah. Why? The sinfulness of man's heart easily subverts the strength of his limbs and brings great wickedness into the world. So, it is the righteousness and simplicity of Noah that garner God's favor. The contrast is telling: the mighty will be brought down and the lowly will be exalted.

Sound familiar? This is the logic that we wait for and find most perfectly displayed at the end of Advent: in choosing to humble himself, taking the form of a slave, God enters the world through a lowly handmaiden and, in so doing, scatters the proud and brings down the powerful from their thrones (see Phil 2:7 and Lk 1:48–52). God's plans are realized through the humble, not the proud, through those who rely on God, not those who think themselves self-sufficient.

Noah gives us an insight into God's humble ways, standing out in the midst of many wayward figures we've encountered up to this point. Genesis tells of Adam and Eve's disobedience, Cain's fratricidal envy, Lamech's bigamous and violent ways, and the wickedness of the mighty men, the men of renown. But Noah offers a contrast that points ahead to Mary and the Incarnation: he demonstrates humble obedience that recognizes the need for God. It is through this obedience that God saves the world—in the case at hand, it is through Noah that the world of humans and animals is saved from the destruction of the flood. And if that isn't a mighty deed, I don't know what is!

About that flood ... Did you notice that the way it's described here takes us back to the very beginning of Genesis? Not directly, but through parallels and echoes: watery chaos, divine utterances, a covenantal form, creatures according to specific kinds, male and female, instructions about food. It's not a creation account, but it *is* the beginning of a re-creation account.

It's a new beginning—and not the first one in Genesis. Our God is not a one-shot God, but a God of second (and third, and fourth ...) chances. We need second chances because we're slow learners; sometimes it takes us more than one time before we really get it. But once we do get it, we realize that following God is not terribly complicated. Sure, there can be some complicated things, but at its heart, it isn't meant to be complicated. I love how the end of the passage above presents this. God does give some detailed instructions—and building an ark isn't exactly small or simple—but after that, we read: "Noah did this; he did all that God commanded him" (Gen 6:22).

It's so simple. But it's all that God asks: to listen to his words and to follow him. This is the obedience we didn't see in the Garden of Eden, nor in the life of Cain, nor, seemingly, anywhere until Noah. Noah obeys, he trusts, he relies on God, on God's plans, and on the instructions that point out the way. As a result, he is righteous, blameless, and free—free from the ravages of the flood, free to live.

Obedience and freedom are two sides of the same coin. We are created in God's image, and the freedom that comes along with this is not unlimited, like the freedom of the Creator. It's limited, because it's the freedom of the creature, requiring direction, formation. The *Catechism* brings out this point nicely: "Human freedom is a force for growth and maturity in truth and goodness; it attains its perfection when directed toward God, our beatitude" (1731).

We are created free, but we grow in freedom by directing it toward God and learning from him. We take time to meditate on God's plan and his instructions in Scripture so that we can shape our freedom properly. We come to the Father in prayer so that we can be shaped by his love, learning to use our freedom for the sake of love.

That is, after all, what freedom is for. We don't seek it for its own sake so that we can be in control, make all the decisions, blaze a trail! Seeking freedom in this way is the contradiction that plagues Adam and Eve,

Cain, Lamech, and all those in the line down to Noah. Through his simple obedience, Noah reminds us that freedom is ordered through obedience to love: love of God, love of neighbor, and love of creation.

Questions for Reflection and Discussion

- You are freely taking time this Advent to work through these Jesse Tree reflections—that's great! But there's more to the day than these few minutes. What more can you give to our Lord to prepare your heart for his coming at Christmas? How about simple obedience in those moments when it seems hardest?

- Has there been a time in your life when you knew what God wanted and you did it easily and promptly? What was the result? What would it be like if you did that more often?

Resolutions to Consider

- When today could you practice simple obedience to the moment and to the demands of the person right in front of you, the task that needs to be completed, the need for love or a kind word?

- Examine your conscience tonight and identify the moments when you practiced simple obedience and those when you sought your own will instead.

- Reflect on what makes it hardest in your life to practice simple obedience, whether a person, place, time, or situation. Commit to one small improvement in this challenge.

Build a Family Tradition

- With your family, read or tell in your own words the story of Noah and the flood in Genesis 6.

- Notice the ideas of water, chaos, covenant, and God's governance. Note the main point: the contrast between the mighty men of the earth and the simplicity of Noah.

- Hang up your Jesse Tree ornament. (Suggested image: Noah's ark)

- Discuss the following: *If Noah accomplished something great, like building an ark, simply by following God's instructions, what great things could we do if we listened to God and followed him?*

Day 6

Babel

The Story of Salvation: Genesis 11:1–9

Now the whole earth had one language and few words. And as men migrated from the east, they found a plain in the land of Shinar and settled there. And they said to one another, "Come, let us make bricks, and burn them thoroughly." And they had brick for stone, and bitumen for mortar. Then they said, "Come, let us build ourselves a city, and a tower with its top in the heavens, and let us make a name for ourselves, lest we be scattered abroad upon the face of the whole earth." And the LORD came down to see the city and the tower, which the sons of men had built. And the LORD said, "Behold, they are one people, and they have all one language; and this is only the beginning of what they will do; and nothing that they propose to do will now be impossible for them. Come, let us go down, and there confuse their language, that they may not understand one another's speech." So

the LORD scattered them abroad from there over the face of all the
earth, and they left off building the city. Therefore its name was
called Ba'bel, because there the LORD confused the language of
all the earth; and from there the LORD scattered them abroad over
the face of all the earth.

A Meditation for Today

I can remember as a child reading the story of Babel in an illustrated Bible and being impressed by the magnificence of the tower. So, when God punishes the people, I thought, "What!? What went wrong here?" To my child's mind, God seemed to be a little petty or even fickle.

Is God petty? It can seem that way because it's almost like God is afraid that the abilities or power of humans—which he gave to them to begin with—will start to threaten his own power. So, he's going to punish them by knocking them down a peg or two? That seems ... well, wrong.

Is God fickle? Again, it could look like that because the people are only doing what God created them to be and to do: to be human, created in God's image, with unique abilities, and to have dominion over the earth and use their intelligence to build, among other things. But then God seems to say, "Well, not like that!"

The story walks a fine line here, not to make us question God but to challenge us to enter into the story, to look really hard to see what's going on: both in the story and our own lives. And if we look closely, I think we can make a strong case that this story is dripping with human pride.

Why build a tower to begin with? Perhaps to avoid being susceptible to a divine punishment like the flood a few chapters earlier. If that's the case, why choose a plain and not start somewhere higher up, like a mountain or plateau? And why use bricks, a product of human craft, rather than wood, a product of divine creation? And how high should this tower be? To the heavens, perhaps so that they can "be like God," as Satan tempted Adam and Eve in the garden. It's hard to avoid the impression that the motivations at work here do not align with God's instruction to have dominion over the earth, which indicates more a sense of stewardship than domination.

But the real kicker is the line, "Let us make a name for ourselves" (Gen 11:4). Of the many sayings that could serve as a slogan for today's world, that one would be a great candidate. Is anything more important than our reputation, our appearance before others, our perfectly curated image on our social media channels?

And how are we to achieve making a name for ourselves? By cleverness and sheer hard work, of course. "We don't need to start on a mountain; we'll build on a plain!" We are to be self-made men and women. We are to be self-reliant. We're to draw from our own resources. "We don't need to use wood when we can make bricks on our own!" We're to pull ourselves up by our proverbial bootstraps. "We'll build to the heavens!"

And if this isn't enough, we bring these same attitudes about the world around us into our spiritual lives. If only I clock this amount of time in prayer, do that novena, go on these retreats ... then interior peace, pious fervor, and radiating sanctity will be *mine*.

Now, hard work is very good, as are our own resources, prayer, retreats, and everything else I've just mentioned, even reputation. So—to return to our story—when the people at Babel hope for a good name, it isn't the name that's the problem. If we ask what is wrong in the phrase "Let us make a name for ourselves," the answer is found in *us* and *for ourselves.* The people of Babel rely on themselves too much and thus practically exclude relying on the Lord—and we do the very same.

There is a deep and dangerous pride at work here that the *Catechism* mentions in connection with Babel. It first points out that God's covenant with Noah foresees various nations, each with its own land, families, and language. It then says: "This state of division into many nations is at once cosmic, social, and religious. It is intended to limit the pride of fallen humanity, united only in its perverse ambition to forge its own unity as at Babel" (57). Pride motivates us to take matters into our own hands and to rely on ourselves, to the exclusion of God and his help. Ultimately, God wants the people of the earth to be united, but this unity cannot be brought about by human power; it can only be brought about by divine power. And this brings us to an illuminating contrast: Babel pridefully asserts, "Let *us* make a name *for ourselves,*" but Abraham, in the next chapter, humbly believes God's promise, "I will ... make your name great" (Gen 12:2). But that's getting a little ahead of ourselves!

With all of this in view, I think we can see that God is neither petty nor fickle. Instead, he is actually merciful and consistent. The punishment is intended as a medicine to counter human pride by helping humans do what God had always intended: that they form nations and spread across the earth.

I hope we can also see how susceptible we are to the same kind of pride that we witness at Babel. We want to take matters into our own hands; we don't really want to rely on God; we'll manage on our own. But like the people at Babel, we deceive ourselves. The season of Advent directs us toward Christ's coming, which demonstrates a humility we so desperately need. Christ is the solution. He is the one who enables us to become "like God"—according to God's plan, not ours. He is the one who will unite all the nations—according to God's plan, not ours.

Questions for Reflection and Discussion

- How important to you is your name, your reputation? Do you flatter, criticize, or stretch the truth to preserve or increase it? Do you ask God to strengthen and preserve your good reputation and then rely on him for success?

- How do you think about the balance between, on the one hand, the need to plan and be resourceful, and, on the other hand, to trust in God and his providence? Do you find you lean more in one direction or the other?

Resolutions to Consider

- In prayer, give over to God a particular challenge related to your reputation at work or elsewhere and tell him you trust him to take care of you.

- Examine your conscience at some point today and try to identify where you are tempted to do something unseemly or wrong for the sake of success or reputation. Ask God for forgiveness and help.

- Commit to saying something today to build up a friend, acquaintance, or coworker rather than yourself.

Build a Family Tradition

- With your family, read or tell in your own words the scene of Babel in Genesis 11.

- Call attention to the motivations that might be at work in the story. Note the main point: the people of Babel try to do things on their own, including reaching the heavens, and God humbles them.

- Hang up your Jesse Tree ornament. (Suggested image: Tower of Babel)

- Discuss the following: *Why would God place limits on our creativity, kind of like he did for the people of Babel?*

Day 7

Radical Faith

The Story of Salvation: Genesis 12:1–7

Now the LORD said to Abram, "Go from your country and your kindred and your father's house to the land that I will show you. And I will make of you a great nation, and I will bless you, and make your name great, so that you will be a blessing. I will bless those who bless you, and him who curses you I will curse; and by you all the families of the earth shall bless themselves."

So Abram went, as the LORD had told him; and Lot went with him. Abram was seventy-five years old when he departed from Haran. And Abram took Sar'ai his wife, and Lot his brother's son, and all their possessions that they had gathered, and the persons that they had gotten in Haran; and they set forth to go to the land of Canaan. When they came to the land of Canaan, Abram passed through the land to the place at She'chem, to the Oak of Mo'reh. At that time the Canaanites were in the land.

Then the LORD appeared to Abram, and said, "To your descendants I will give this land." So he built there an altar to the LORD, who had appeared to him.

A Meditation for Today

Genesis is a book about origins—that's what the name means. We've heard about the origins of the world, the origins of human beings, the origins of sin, the origins of arts and crafts, the origins of languages and nations. So, when we get to the story of Abram, it's striking that chapter 12 opens with no account of Abram's origins! We don't read it here, but chapter 11 ends with a genealogy that includes Abram, but we don't really know anything about Abram himself—his childhood, his views of the world, his motivations, or even his religion.

Out of nowhere, God gives an instruction to Abram—and that's the beginning of the story. "Go from your country and your kindred and your father's house to the land that I will show you" (Gen 12:1). Does Abram have a past? Undoubtedly. But here's the thing: he is fundamentally a man defined by the future and by the invitation to step into that future with God.

We all have a past, and we carry it with us in many ways. But, like Abram, when we commit ourselves to following the Lord, we are at the most fundamental level defined by that loving invitation. We are no longer the sum of our past experiences but rather—as Saint John Paul II once said—"the sum of the Father's love for us" and of the future that his loving call opens before us.

To say yes to the Father's love for us is comforting, but to say, in the same breath, yes to God's invitation to follow wherever his love will lead us can be ... unsettling. It puts us in a position very similar to Abram's. What God has in store, we know not; where he will call us, we see not; what the cost will be, we fathom not. This is the venture of faith, the adventure of discipleship. It is the noble and daring business of saying yes to the Lord's invitation and following him wherever he leads.

Life with God is a venture, a risk, and walking alongside Abram can teach us something about the course and cost of this path. The first thing to say about this course is that seeing it and setting out on it begins with faith. The *Catechism* speaks of Abraham (as Abram is known after God changes his name in Gen 17:5) as the "father of all who believe" and a model of faith: "The Letter to the Hebrews ... lays special emphasis on Abraham's faith: 'By faith, Abraham obeyed when he was called to go out to a place which he was to receive as an inheritance; and he went out, not knowing where he was to go' (Heb 11:8)" (145). This is the scene we've read today. But the *Catechism* goes on: "By faith, he lived as a stranger and pilgrim in the promised land. By faith, Sarah was given to conceive the son of the promise. And by faith Abraham offered his only son in sacrifice."

Abraham's whole life is built upon faith and characterized by it—and so too the Christian life. This faith is no mere human belief. It is a supernatural reality we call a theological virtue. The theological virtue of faith is a gift given by God and poured into the soul that lifts up the mind and sets before it new vistas of who God is and what his loving plan for us is. It believes in God and everything that he says, for he is truth itself.

Faith accepts and sees into the mystery of God—it does not do away with the mystery, nor does it see perfectly all that God has in store for us. And this is why the life of faith is an adventure and involves risk. Are you willing to take a risk for Christ? Are you willing, as Saint John Henry Newman once said, to venture something for God? Of course, it shouldn't be an imprudent or irresponsible risk—like selling the house your family lives in on a whim! Instead, is there something small you could do that shows a radical trust in God? Can you venture fifteen, twenty, or thirty minutes a day in prayer? Can you "throw away" that productive time? Can you "waste" a little bit of sleep or that precious morning time before the children are up, for example? Is there something—it needn't be huge—something that the "world" would look at and consider a puzzling waste or risk but that you are willing to undertake out of faith in God and his promises?

I bet there is. Every adventure includes some risk, and Advent is the perfect time to recommit to the adventure of faith. Even the words are similar: Advent and adventure. The root meaning has to do with something coming toward us. In Advent, Christ draws near, and what he will offer to us is an adventure, something that we don't seek out but that comes toward us, befalls us, and sweeps us away. So, like Abram, let us take up the adventure the Lord has put before us, and let us be willing to stake our lives on the faith we profess.

Questions for Reflection and Discussion

- What are you willing to venture or risk for God? What have you done recently that shows radical trust in him?

- Recall a time when you trusted God and set out on a new path. What difference did that make in your life? What consequences do you still experience today?

- Think of a favorite saint and how his or her life showed radical trust in God. What lessons could you apply to your own life?

Resolutions to Consider

- Pick one comfort that the "world" says is desirable or even necessary and give it up for today ... and maybe tomorrow, too!

- Set aside extra time for prayer today, sacrificing something else you might have been looking forward to.

- Commit to doing one good thing today, maybe something you've been putting off, that goes beyond your comfort zone and requires a little more courage than usual.

Build a Family Tradition

- With your family, read or tell in your own words the story of Abram and his invitation to follow God in Genesis 12.

- Feel the weight of the invitation that comes out of the blue. Note the main point: God invites, Abram says yes, and God takes care of him.

- Hang up your Jesse Tree ornament. (Suggested image: walking stick)

- Discuss the following: *Abram's invitation was a long time ago, but how does God still invite us to follow him today?*

Day 8

Father and Son

The Story of Salvation: Genesis 22:1–8

After these things God tested Abraham, and said to him, "Abraham!" And he said, "Here I am." He said, "Take your son, your only-begotten son Isaac, whom you love, and go to the land of Mori'ah, and offer him there as a burnt offering upon one of the mountains of which I shall tell you." So Abraham rose early in the morning, saddled his donkey, and took two of his young men with him, and his son Isaac; and he cut the wood for the burnt offering, and arose and went to the place of which God had told him. On the third day Abraham lifted up his eyes and saw the place afar off. Then Abraham said to his young men, "Stay here with the donkey; I and the lad will go yonder and worship, and come again to you." And Abraham took the wood of the burnt offering, and laid it on Isaac his son; and he took in his hand the fire and the knife. So they went both of them together. And Isaac said to his father Abraham, "My father!" And he said, "Here I am, my son." He said, "Behold, the fire and the wood; but where is the lamb for a burnt offering?" Abraham said, "God will provide himself the lamb for a burnt offering, my son." So they went both of them together.

A Meditation for Today

Does God ask the impossible of us? Yes! And, no. How can that be?

In a section on the meaning of faith, the *Catechism* holds up Abraham as a model of faith, the "'father of all who believe'" (146). It then goes on to point to Mary as the perfect embodiment of faith (148). Why does it pair Abraham and Mary? Think about how similar their situations are: at a general level, both are going about their business when God shows up and asks something of each that requires faith. And not just any faith, but radical faith. To get more specific: of Abraham, God asks that he sacrifice his beloved son; of Mary, God asks that she be the Mother of God. In both cases, there is a kind of contradiction, and what God says is to be done appears to be impossible. God has promised Abraham that he will be the father of many nations through his son Isaac, but then he asks for Isaac's life. God promises Mary that she will give birth to the Son of God, but she is also to remain a virgin. Both Abraham and Mary have such great faith that they can accept what God says even when it presents what seems to be an impossibility.

It is impossible for Abraham to generate descendants through Isaac if he first sacrifices Isaac's life; likewise, it is impossible for Mary to generate new life if she "[has] no husband." Both of these are completely impossible ... for human beings.

Not for God. Abraham knows this, and for this reason, one line of his is especially important: "God will provide himself the lamb for a burnt offering," in Genesis 22:8. Mary knows this, too, and so she asks, in Luke 1:34, "How will this be ... ?" rather than questioning "Can this be ... ?" Both Abraham and Mary know that what is impossible for humans can be possible for God.

Let's focus again on Abraham and his affirmation that "God will provide the lamb." In the season of Advent, we hear in this line a foreshadowing of what God will do at Christmas: he sends his Son among us, the Lamb of God who takes away the sins of the world. And because God the Father is willing to send his Son into the world to die for us, Abraham and Isaac foreshadow this great mystery—father and son, both pointing ahead to our heavenly Father and his beloved Son.

But we should also hear in this line the depth of Abraham's faith, enriched and enlivened by hope and love. He believes God, and he believes what God says. But if what God promises is impossible for Abraham to bring about, shouldn't Abraham despair of ever accomplishing it? No, for "God will provide himself." Not only does Abraham have *faith* in what God says, he also has *hope*, trusting in God's promises to bring it about, and he has *love*, being willing to go through with it, to give all that he has out of love for God and his plan of salvation.

Faith needs these two other theological virtues, hope and love, in order to reach its full perfection. Without hope, we'd know what God has revealed, but we'd be left to despair of ever accomplishing it. Without love, we'd look upon what God has said with a kind of distance and coldness rather than desiring it, embracing it, and delighting in it.

Abraham's dilemma might seem to us both distant and sort of extreme, like we can't really relate to it. But in it we actually find an icon of the whole Christian proposition: God reveals to us that we are invited to enter into a loving communion with him for eternity. We believe him in faith but realize that it is a natural impossibility for us—of our own resources, we could never reach supernatural happiness. It is hope that saves us from despair, trusting that God will accomplish what he has promised. And love draws us ever closer to this heavenly good; it makes us long for it and unites us with it.

The season of Advent leads us to the beginning of God's fulfillment of his promise to save us and to make us his adopted children through grace. And the theological virtues of faith, hope, and love are the distinctive marks of our life as children of God. As the *Catechism* says, "They are infused by God into the souls of the faithful to make them capable of acting as his children and of meriting eternal life" (1813).

Advent is the perfect time to strengthen these virtues as we wait for Christ. Although they are given by God, we can still cultivate them in various ways. Faith can be bolstered by continuing to learn about the mysteries of salvation and how these transform our life. Hope can be fortified by expressing gratitude to God and asking him for the things we need to do his will, because prayer is an act of hope in God. And love can be increased simply by spending time with our beloved, with

God—talking with him, thinking about him, and receiving his love, which enkindles our own.

Questions for Reflection and Discussion

- We often don't fully appreciate the fact that salvation is absolutely impossible for us to attain on our own. If you take this seriously, what consequences can you draw from it?

- Has there been a time in your life when God seemed to be asking you to sacrifice something dear to you? How did you respond? What did you learn from it?

Resolutions to Consider

- Pick one theological virtue, pray for God to strengthen it, and commit to doing one thing to deepen that virtue of faith, hope, or love.

- Perform an act of loving service for someone close to you today.

- Tell God in prayer that you will rely on him more in a current situation in your life—and then actually do it.

Build a Family Tradition

- With your family, read or tell in your own words the story of Abraham and Isaac in Genesis 22.

- Pay special attention to the language and details. Acknowledge that the passage is mysterious in many ways, but what seems clear is that Abraham trusts God above all things.

- Hang up your Jesse Tree ornament. (Suggested image: wood for fire)

- Discuss the following: *God asks Abraham to give up something very precious—could he ask something similar of us, and why might he do that?*

Day 9

Wrestling with God

The Story of Salvation: Genesis 32:22–31

The same night he arose and took his two wives, his two maids, and his eleven children, and crossed the ford of the Jabbok. He took them and sent them across the stream, and likewise everything that he had. And Jacob was left alone; and a man wrestled with him until the breaking of the day. When the man saw that he did not prevail against Jacob, he touched the hollow of his thigh; and Jacob's thigh was put out of joint as he wrestled with him. Then he said, "Let me go, for the day is breaking." But Jacob said, "I will not let you go, unless you bless me." And he said to him, "What is your name?" And he said, "Jacob." Then he said, "Your name shall no more be called Jacob, but Israel, for you have striven with God and with men, and have prevailed." Then Jacob asked him, "Tell me, I pray, your name." But he said, "Why is it that you ask my name?" And there he blessed him. So

Jacob called the name of the place Peni´el, saying, "For I have seen God face to face, and yet my life is preserved." The sun rose upon him as he passed Penu´el, limping because of his thigh.

A Meditation for Today

What kind of a man is Jacob? He is . . . a wrestler! Even when he was a baby in the womb, Genesis describes him as a wrestler. Back in Genesis 25, Rebekah is pregnant with twins, and it says of her pregnancy, "The children struggled together within her" (Gen 25:22). And then at birth, Esau is born first, but Jacob is born holding his heel—in other words, in the middle of some neonatal jujitsu. But it doesn't stop there. We find out that later in life Jacob still loves wrestling—he falls in love with a woman who has wrestling on her mind. You didn't know that, did you? It's true! Rachel and Leah are competing for Jacob's love, and, in Genesis 30, Rachel says, "With mighty wrestlings I have wrestled with my sister, and have prevailed" (Gen 30:8). So, when we get to the passage we read today, Genesis 32, it isn't surprising that we find Jacob once again in the midst of his life's passion: wrestling, this time with an angel.

If this seems like a lot of attention given to wrestling, there's a reason for it: wrestling involves grasping; it includes leveraging; it expresses trying to force your will on your opponent. And all of this characterizes who Jacob is and what he does. He grasps after his father's blessing. He leverages Esau's hunger to make him sell his birthright. He forces his will on Isaac and Esau by taking advantage of Isaac's blindness, deceiving him about his identity, and stealing the blessing of the firstborn. He does whatever it takes to win his wife, Rachel, from Laban. He applies his cleverness and craftiness to make himself wealthy from Laban's flocks, at Laban's expense. He then uses all of his planning and resourcefulness to try to placate Esau when he meets him for the first time many years after stealing his blessing.

So, when Jacob wrestles in Genesis 32, it's a scene symbolic of who he is and how he's lived his life. But it's also a scene of transformation. There are so many fascinating details here, but I want to focus on two things. First, as Jacob wrestles his opponent, the two seem evenly matched. By the end of the confrontation, it still isn't entirely clear who the winner is: Jacob suffers a debilitating blow that leaves him limping, and then, still holding on, he asks for a blessing. Both of these moments suggest the superiority of his opponent. But it's the other man, or angel, who asks to be let go and then describes Jacob as having prevailed. It's as though Jacob wins by losing. It's very mysterious!

The second point is what I think marks the decisive moment: when Jacob's opponent asks him his name. Jacob has been asked before who he is by Isaac—and he lied in reply: "I am Esau your first-born" (Gen 27:19). But now, he responds truthfully, simply: "Jacob." With that, he acknowledges for the first time his true identity: I am Jacob, the heel catcher, the grasping one, the deceiver, the trickster. It's a confession of sorts, and only through this confession does Jacob receive a divine blessing, a new name, and a new role: the wrestler becomes a patriarch.

This doesn't mean he leaves wrestling behind. It stays with him, and it might surprise you to learn that it stays with us, too. In its section on prayer, the *Catechism* points to a long-standing tradition of seeing in Jacob's wrestling a depiction of prayer. Prayer is a gift, but it's also a struggle, a wrestling match. "Jacob wrestles all night with a mysterious figure who refuses to reveal his name but who blesses him before leaving him at dawn. From this account, the spiritual tradition of the Church has retained the symbol of prayer as a battle of faith and as the triumph of perseverance" (2573).

The lesson in perseverance is clear: through the ups and downs of prayer, we have to stick with it, never giving up. But as for the battle of faith, part of that is learning to be honest before God. Just as Jacob has to learn to confess who he truly is—the grasping one—we also have to learn to do the same. In prayer, we come before God in humility, acknowledging who we truly are: we are … Jacob, or at least his spiritual heirs. We are sinners who grasp for things beyond our reach. But we are also adopted sons and daughters of God, who are learning to rely on him to give us all that we need and more. And like Jacob, we win in prayer by losing: losing our old selves by confessing who we truly are; losing our exaggerated self-reliance by learning to limp alongside the God who supports us.

So, thinking about prayer, we have to ask ourselves: am I honest with God in prayer? Do I pretend to be the person I think God wants me to be instead of acknowledging in prayer the person I actually am? True prayer always begins in humility, acknowledging our need for God, our reliance on him, rather than grasping after the things we want, turning all circumstances to our will instead of praying, "thy will be done."

Advent is the perfect time to reflect on all this because we look ahead to the one foreshadowed by Jacob: Jesus, who will demonstrate the ultimate version of winning by losing. Through his death on the cross, he conquers death and rises to new life, bringing us along with him.

Questions for Reflection and Discussion

- Consider how honest, straightforward, and simple you are with God in prayer. Are you tempted at certain moments or in certain situations to be less than perfectly straightforward with God?

- Outside of prayer, when do you experience the temptation to be like Jacob, grasping after things, using all of your natural abilities and resources to direct things in your favor; being overly clever, possibly to the point of dishonesty?

Resolutions to Consider

- Spend ten minutes in prayer just talking to God in your own words, with honesty and simplicity.

- Find one moment today to be especially straightforward with someone close to you—it can be a positive thing, too, like telling someone very simply and without pretense, "I love you" or "I really appreciate . . . about you."

Build a Family Tradition

- With your family, read or tell in your own words the account of Jacob and the wrestling episode in Genesis 32.

- Draw attention to the funny way the wrestling match ends with no clear winner. Note the main point: for the first time, Jacob confesses who he truly is.

- Hang up your Jesse Tree ornament. (Suggested image: Jacob's Ladder)

- Discuss the following: *How is prayer sometimes like wrestling?*

Day 10

The Work of Mercy

The Story of Salvation: Genesis 45:1–8

Then Joseph could not control himself before all those who stood by him; and he cried, "Make everyone go out from me." So no one stayed with him when Joseph made himself known to his brothers. And he wept aloud, so that the Egyptians heard it, and the household of Pharaoh heard it. And Joseph said to his brothers, "I am Joseph; is my father still alive?" But his brothers could not answer him, for they were dismayed at his presence.

So Joseph said to his brothers, "Come near to me, I beg you." And they came near. And he said, "I am your brother, Joseph, whom you sold into Egypt. And now do not be distressed, or angry with yourselves, because you sold me here; for God sent me before you to preserve life. For the famine has been in the land these two years; and there are yet five years in which there will be neither plowing nor harvest. And God sent me before you to preserve for you a remnant on earth, and to keep alive for you many survivors. So it was not you who sent me here, but God; And he has made me a father to Pharaoh, and lord of all his house and ruler over all the land of Egypt."

A Meditation for Today

I remember as a child being introduced to the musical *Joseph and the Amazing Technicolor Dreamcoat* by Andrew Lloyd Webber and Tim Rice. Sure, the libretto isn't always biblically accurate ... nor is it the most theologically profound ... but the music is creative, it's fun, and, most importantly, it's remarkably, even comically, varied. The emotional range of the songs really brought out an important truth: life has its ups and downs—and I think no story in the Bible illustrates this more clearly than the story of the Old Testament patriarch Joseph.

He is lifted up by his father's favor to a special place in the family; he's given a special coat; he's gifted with dreams and the ability to interpret them. But, things go awry and Joseph ends up falling into deep disfavor with his brothers; he's stripped of his coat, thrown down into a pit, and sold into slavery. But then he rises through the ranks in Egypt, finding favor with Potiphar, before he again sinks to new lows when he is imprisoned on false charges. But finally, he comes to Pharaoh's attention and reaches new highs in favor, position, and power. This is not your ordinary story—it's like a roller coaster ride, with its twists and turns, its ups and downs.

Despite the wild twists and turns, the story also reveals patterns that remain constant. One pattern, a really important one, is God's faithfulness and his closeness to Joseph. While Joseph is in Egypt, the Lord is said to be with him over and over again. He's with him in his highest moments, as the root cause of his successes, and in his lowest moments, as a comfort and a promise of future redemption.

Another pattern is one we've already talked about: the pendulum swings of Joseph's fortunes rising and falling. From father's favor to slavery, from managing Potiphar's household to prison, and then from there to Pharaoh's right hand. It is at that point, in the height of his power that Joseph comes into contact again with his brothers ... and this leads us to the passage we just read above.

After testing his brothers to see whether they've mended their ways, Joseph reveals his identity to them. Not only that, he reveals his intentions as well: not to take vengeance on them but to provide for them. Finally, he also reveals God's ways to them, at least as he understands them: God allowed all of the ups and downs, the twists and turns, so that Joseph could end up in a position of power where he could take care of his family and preserve their lives in the midst of famine.

What the whole family has learned, from Jacob to the last of his sons, is that God works all things for good. Why? Not because he is forced to do so, but because he chooses to do so out of mercy: seeing our need, our weakness, our affliction, our sin, God comes to our aid to bring about good.

Joseph teaches his family, and us, about God's merciful ways. And not only that, he models that we should respond in turn. In his moment of greatest power and, in a sense, triumph—everything has come full circle in the scene we read—Joseph uses his position and power to show mercy.

Especially in the midst of our successes, we should do the same: show mercy to those around us, responding to someone's need by being moved at heart … and not just moved, but moved to action. Mercy involves both being moved at heart and moved to action. We serve those in need, working to remedy what is lacking and bring about good.

Although the works of mercy are innumerable, the *Catechism* hands down to us what we traditionally call the spiritual and corporal works of mercy: "Charitable actions by which we come to the aid of our neighbor in his spiritual and bodily necessities" (2447). It lists teaching, advising, consoling, comforting, forgiving, and bearing wrongs patiently as spiritual works of mercy. Notice how many of these Joseph demonstrates in the scene we read: in the presence of his brothers, he teaches them, advises them, consoles them, comforts them, forgives them, and bears their earlier wrongs with patience. The corporal works of mercy include feeding the hungry, giving drink to the thirsty, sheltering the homeless, clothing the naked, visiting the sick and imprisoned, giving alms to the poor, and burying the dead. These too are amply demonstrated by Joseph in the final chapters (42–50) of the book of Genesis: feeding his family during the famine, giving drink to his brothers in Egypt, providing shelter for them in Egypt, giving them money to take back home, likely visiting Simeon in prison and freeing him, and then burying his father after he dies.

Joseph is a kind of icon of mercy, and in this way he points to Christ, who is the merciful one par excellence, even mercy incarnate. As we draw closer to Christ's coming in Advent, we wait for his merciful intervention with hearts full of love and anticipation. And because we know that we receive mercy, let's recommit ourselves to showing mercy to others, especially through the spiritual and corporal works of mercy.

Questions for Reflection and Discussion

- Where do you find yourself at this very moment? Maybe it's an "up" moment—if so, how can you share this fullness by showing mercy to someone close to you? Or it could be a "down" moment—if that's the case, ask God for his mercy and then look for it, because it won't be long in coming, though it can appear different than we imagine.

- What comes to mind when you think of God's mercy? What other ways or moments exemplify his mercy in your life?

Resolutions to Consider

- Pick a spiritual or corporal work of mercy and commit to performing it at least once this week.

- Think of someone you need to forgive, forgive this person today, and then tell them you've forgiven them.

- If you have children, practice viewing the things you do for them through the lens of mercy—being moved at heart because of some lack they have and then providing what is lacking.

Build a Family Tradition

- With your family, read or tell in your own words the narrative about Joseph, which culminates in Genesis 45.

- Point out how unconventional Joseph's path is, but highlight the main point as well: God is faithful in each of these moments and ultimately uses them for good.

- Hang up your Jesse Tree ornament. (Suggested image: Joseph's multicolored coat)

- Discuss the following: *What can Joseph's life teach us about God's ways and trusting in his plan?*

Day 11

A Great Invitation

The Story of Salvation: Exodus 3:1–2, 4–7, 10–14

Now Moses was keeping the flock of his father-in-law, Jethro, the priest of Mid'ian; and he led his flock to the west side of the wilderness, and came to Horeb, the mountain of God. And the angel of the LORD appeared to him in a flame of fire out of the midst of a bush; and he looked, and behold, the bush was burning, yet it was not consumed. ... God called to him out of the bush, "Moses, Moses!" And he said, "Here am I." Then he said, "Do not come near; put off your shoes from your feet, for the place on which you are standing is holy ground." And he said, "I am the God of your father, the God of Abraham, the God of Isaac, and the God of Jacob." And Moses hid his face, for he was afraid to look at God.

Then the LORD said, "I have seen the affliction of my people who are in Egypt, and have heard their cry because of their taskmasters. I know their sufferings ... Come, I will send you to Pharaoh that you may bring forth my people, the sons of Israel, out of Egypt." But Moses said to God, "Who am I that I should go to Pharaoh, and bring the sons of Israel out of Egypt?" He said, "But I will be with you; and this shall be the sign for you, that I have sent you: when you have brought forth the people out of Egypt, you shall serve God upon this mountain."

Then Moses said to God, "If I come to the sons of Israel and say to them, 'The God of your fathers has sent me to you,' and they ask me, 'What is his name?' what shall I say to them?" God said to Moses, "I AM WHO I AM." And he said, "Say this to the sons of Israel: 'I AM has sent me to you.'"

A Meditation for Today

The burning bush is like an introduction of sorts: Moses, I'm God—the God of your father, of Abraham, Isaac, and Jacob. And what an introduction! Not surprisingly, Moses is stunned. He's in awe. He hides his face because he's afraid to look at God. But this is just the beginning of a remarkable story of friendship between God and Moses. By the end of the book, Moses no longer hides his face. He'll speak to God face-to-face, as with a friend. He knows him intimately, knows who God is—merciful, loving, patient, steadfast, forgiving (see Ex 34). But here at the beginning, Moses is introduced to God and God reveals his mysterious name to Moses: I AM WHO I AM, or, as it can also be translated, I AM WHO I WILL BE.

And then comes an astonishing invitation: Go to Egypt, confront the most powerful ruler, whose power is built on the back of Hebrew slaves, and ask him to set those slaves free. If that isn't a monumental task, I don't know what is! God calls Moses to a great—a herculean—undertaking, and with that, he invites him to magnanimity.

Magna-what? Magnanimity. It means "greatness of soul" or spirit. It's a virtue that prompts us to strive for great things. This is what Moses is asked to do, and this is the virtue he needs to do it.

And he does it! You know the story: God asks Moses, Moses hesitates, God turns out to be pretty persuasive, Moses says yes, one thing leads to another, and—voilà!—the people are free. No, actually it's very complicated, dramatic, and simply tremendous. In fact, it's kind of *the* defining event of the Old Testament: the Exodus.

And *that* can make us think that magnanimity is only for such climactic events and for history-changing individuals like Moses. But that's not true—it's actually a virtue we all need. Because we also are challenged to strive for great things, to be magnanimous!

Which can make us a little uncomfortable. Why? Well, first of all, you might have noticed that, in our little corner of the world, we are practically drowning in comfort and convenience. I'm sure we all have moments where we feel like we don't have as much as others, as much as we'd like, and all that. But the simple truth is that we have far more comforts and conveniences than any generation in history. And so, we tend to settle for ease and pleasure instead of greatness. We like the familiar and the comfortable; we like our routines, our comfort zone. And when greatness comes knocking at our door, we hesitate; we resist it.

This is what Moses did. Even after being awed by the burning bush, when invited on a great mission, he hems and haws; he makes excuses; he tries almost everything to stay in his familiar, comfortable life in Midian. So, we're not alone in preferring comfort to greatness. We're just like Moses.

But here's what Pope Benedict XVI said about this, and it's one of my favorite quotations: "The ways of the Lord are not comfortable, but then again we're not created for comfort; rather, we're created for greatness, for the good … Jesus didn't promise us a comfortable life. And if we come to him looking for comfort, we've come to the wrong place. But he shows us the way to greatness, to goodness, to a truly human life" (Address to German Pilgrims, April 25, 2005).

The Christian life isn't meant to be comfortable, but it is meant to be great. What is the greatness each of us is called to? I don't know—that's the exciting part! What God asks of each of us will be different. But one thing will be the same: he asks us to be his adopted sons and daughters, to be children of the Most High and Glorious King, to be imitators of Christ, the most perfect and remarkable person who ever walked the face of the earth. And this is the invitation to greatness that each of us is invited to say yes to.

We might have another worry: "Aren't we supposed to be humble? And all this about greatness … " Moses also shows us the answer here, or actually, God does. How will Moses accomplish this monumental feat of the Exodus? God gives the answer: "I will be with you." The kind of greatness that God asks of us is only possible because he is with us, helping us. And that mysterious name that God reveals to Moses, I AM WHO I AM or I AM WHO I WILL BE? It can also mean I AM THE ONE WHO WILL BE WITH YOU.

Amazing—"I will be with you." In Advent, we look forward to something even more amazing: God enacts "I will be with you" by sending his Son, Emmanuel, which means "God with us." This is the ultimate fulfillment of who God says he is to Moses: I AM WHO I AM, I AM THE ONE WHO IS WITH YOU—that's who I am. God is with us; he is *within* us, by the presence of his Holy Spirit. This presence and this power within us is what enables us to live out magnanimity and to achieve greatness in Christ. What does this greatness look like? Most of all, it looks like great love. To love *greatly*, no matter the deed, situation, or circumstances, is true Christian magnanimity. And when we learn to do that, who knows what great things will follow.

Questions for Reflection and Discussion

- How to start down the path of Christian greatness? It's best to start ... small, with Saint Thérèse of Lisieux's "little way": to do the little, ordinary things with great love. How can you practice great love in the ordinary?

- How aware are you that God is always with you? How could you increase this awareness?

Resolutions to Consider

- Make a decision to notice when you are hesitating today before doing something good—and then just do it courageously.

- Identify a comfort you might be attached to. Give it up for today.

- Examine your conscience tonight and think of when you are most likely to back down before a significant opportunity. Ask for the grace to embrace the next opportunity.

Build a Family Tradition

- With your family, read or tell in your own words the story of Moses meeting God in Exodus 3.

- Point out how Moses hesitates, how huge the invitation is, and how God promises to support Moses.

- Hang up your Jesse Tree ornament. (Suggested image: burning bush)

- Discuss the following: *Does it make you excited or fearful to be called to greatness, like Moses? A little of both?*

Day 12

The Shape of Love

The Story of Salvation: Exodus 20:1–10, 12–17

And God spoke all these words, saying,

"I am the LORD your God, who brought you out of the land of Egypt, out of the house of bondage.

"You shall have no other gods before me.

"You shall not make for yourself a graven image, or any likeness of anything that is in heaven above, or that is in the earth beneath, or that is in the water under the earth; you shall not bow down to them or serve them; for I the LORD your God am a jealous God, visiting the iniquity of the fathers upon the children to the third and the fourth generation of those who hate me, but showing mercy to thousands of those who love me and keep my commandments.

*"You shall not take the name of the L*ORD *your God in vain; for the Lord will not hold him guiltless who takes his name in vain.*

*"Remember the Sabbath day, to keep it holy. Six days you shall labor, and do all your work; but the seventh day is a Sabbath to the L*ORD *your God; ...*

*"Honor your father and your mother, that your days may be long in the land which the L*ORD *your God gives you.*

"You shall not kill.

"You shall not commit adultery.

"You shall not steal.

"You shall not bear false witness against your neighbor.

"You shall not covet your neighbor's house; you shall not covet your neighbor's wife, or his manservant, or his maidservant, or his ox, or his donkey, or anything that is your neighbor's."

A Meditation for Today

How are the covenant and the Promised Land linked in the Ten Commandments? Well, occupying a land is of little value unless the people really live as God's Chosen People, which means according to God's covenant. Otherwise, they would be just like the other nations when, in fact, they are meant to be a nation set apart, a holy nation and a light to the other nations.

A high bar, no doubt, but God doesn't leave his people alone to figure it all out on their own. How should they live? What do the ways of the Lord look like for his Chosen People? The Ten Commandments form the core of the answer to these questions. But they do this within the context of a relationship between God and his people, a covenant.

This is a critical point because we tend to think of the Ten Commandments as simply rules or laws. The two tablets of stone emphasize the legal dimension: we think of a code of law written in stone. But when we do this, we're putting the cart before the horse. We're making primary what is in fact secondary. Now, I'm not saying that the commandments or laws don't matter—they do! But as the *Catechism* says, "The Commandments properly so-called come in the second place: they express the implications of belonging to God through the establishment of the covenant. Moral existence is a *response* to the Lord's loving initiative" (2062).

This idea is captured in the very first line of the Ten Commandments, one we tend to overlook: "I am the Lord your God, who brought you out of the land of Egypt, out of the house of bondage" (Ex 20:2). Before God gives any of the "You shall"s and "You shall not"s, he first reminds the people who he is and what he's done for them. His loving action has gone first, and it invites and calls forth a love and a gratitude that look for ways to respond in turn. The commandments are meant to elicit and shape that response. What should love of God look like? It looks like the first three commandments. What should love of neighbor—the neighbor that God has given me by calling us into the same covenant with him—look like? It looks like the last seven commandments.

This looks good on paper—or stone, I suppose—but, of course, all this proves to be more difficult than one might expect: it turns out to be easier to take the people out of Egypt than to take Egypt out of the people. But in a way this shouldn't surprise us. Remember, if the Exodus is God's definitive saving act in the Old Testament and Moses' greatest act, it is definitely an act of magnanimity. And if the Decalogue (the Ten Commandments) outlines a response to that act, then keeping it is also a big deal, a great act. In a way, we could say that the people are invited to participate in God's great act of magnanimity by following the Ten Commandments. God frees the people *from* Egypt and *for* holiness, and that second part requires the cooperation and the agency of the people. To cooperate with God and honor the Ten Commandments is a great and noble act.

For us, too, living out the Ten Commandments is an act of magnanimity. In fact, it is such a great act that we look to Jesus, the perfect man, to demonstrate what that looks like. And it looks like putting God first. It looks like following his holy will. It looks like loving him above all things. It looks like loving and serving our neighbors. It looks ... hard. Really hard.

And it is. But, we also look to Christ to make it possible for us. Only with his help, his grace, are we able to follow the Ten Commandments wholeheartedly. And when we do, we will experience the same peace and joy that Jesus did in keeping the Father's will, even in the most difficult moments.

At the end of Advent, God sends us his Son and he does this to provide the model and the assistance we need for living out the commandments.

So, look to Jesus and ask him to help reshape your love according to his commandments.

Questions for Reflection and Discussion

- Look at the commandments again and try to see them as the shape our love for God should take. Or as the conditions of being in a covenant with him. Or as the various dimensions of our love for God. Then ask yourself: Which of these dimensions is most challenging right now? Which requires God's divine assistance the most?

- Have you considered very often that "all the rules" are given to us in order to make us holy and happy? How can this realization change how you relate to obeying the commandments?

Resolutions to Consider

- Ask yourself which of the Ten Commandments presents the greatest challenge right now, and then commit to performing one deed that helps fulfill that commandment. Perhaps that means confessing a sin, performing an act of love, etc.

- Use the Ten Commandments as an examination of conscience and then commit to going to confession this week.

- Memorize the Ten Commandments.

Build a Family Tradition

- With your family, read or tell in your own words the account of God giving the Ten Commandments in Exodus 20.

- Call attention to the main division of the commandments: the first three relate to God, the last seven relate to our neighbor. Note the main point: God recalls his saving work in the Exodus and then outlines what a response of love looks like.

- Hang up your Jesse Tree ornament. (Suggested image: stone tablets)

- Discuss the following: *Why does God give commandments to his Chosen People and also to us?*

Day 13

Obstacles Within

The Story of Salvation: Joshua 1:1–9

After the death of Moses the servant of the LORD, the LORD said to Joshua the son of Nun, Moses' minister, "Moses my servant is dead; now therefore arise, go over this Jordan, you and all this people, into the land which I am giving to them, to the sons of Israel. Every place that the sole of your foot will tread upon I have given to you, as I promised to Moses. From the wilderness and this Lebanon as far as the great river, the river Euphra'tes, all the land of the Hittites to the Great Sea toward the going down of the sun shall be your territory. No man shall be able to stand before you all the days of your life; as I was with Moses, so I will be with you; I will not fail you or forsake you. Be strong and of good courage; for you shall cause this people to inherit the land which I swore to their fathers to give them. Only be strong and very courageous, being careful to do according to all the law which Moses my servant commanded you; turn not from it to the right hand or to the left, that you may have good success wherever you go. This Book of the Law shall not depart from your mouth, but you shall meditate on it day and night, that you may be careful to do according to all that is written in it; for then you will make your way prosperous, and then you will have good success. Have I not commanded you? Be strong and of good courage; be not frightened, neither be dismayed; for the LORD your God is with you wherever you go."

A Meditation for Today

When God first revealed himself to Moses, he had to convince Moses that he, God, would truly be with him. After God's mighty deeds and steadfast love, Moses comes to believe this wholeheartedly. Joshua seems to have learned the lesson well from Moses. Joshua is almost the embodiment of "the LORD is with us." In the book of Numbers, chapter 13, Joshua is sent with a group to spy out the land of Canaan before they try to occupy it. Upon returning, some in the group despair of conquering the land, and they sow fear and dissension among the people. But Joshua and Caleb rally the people by reminding them of a fundamental truth in Numbers 14:8–9: "If the LORD delights in us, he will bring us into this land and give it to us, a land which flows with milk and honey … The LORD is with us; do not fear them." The Lord is with us—what God promised Moses back at the burning bush remains true, and Joshua shows his utter confidence in this. Success is assured because the Lord is with us.

In the passage above, as Joshua prepares to lead the people into the Promised Land, the same theme rings out: "The LORD your God is with you wherever you go," and it is because Joshua takes this to heart that success is sure to follow.

If this is the case, we might wonder why the overall tenor of the passage seems so … ominous? How many times does God remind Joshua to be strong, to be not afraid, to have courage? It's quite a few! But if God is with him, then what would tempt him to lose heart, to be fearful, to give up? What sort of obstacles might arise? They *must* be difficult if they require such courage.

Some of the most difficult obstacles are not the ones that come from the outside but from within. Internal obstacles—like unfaithfulness, despair, presumption, lukewarmness, indifference, laziness—are the greatest dangers and temptations that God's people face.

We face them, too. In fact, the *Catechism* lists all of the sins I just mentioned as sins against the theological virtues of faith, hope, and love. It talks about incredulity, or lack of faith, as being opposed to faith, obviously (2089). It mentions despair and presumption as sins against hope (see 2091–92). And it covers lukewarmness, indifference, and laziness as failures in love (2094).

How can we overcome the temptations that lead to these sins? By taking to heart God's reminder to Joshua: "The LORD your God is with you wherever you go." And for us baptized believers, this assurance takes on an even more profound and intimate meaning. We talked earlier about the theological virtues, and it's important to realize and remember that these are God's very presence within us, perfecting us. The *Catechism* says that these virtues "are infused by God into the souls of the faithful to make them capable of acting as his children … They are the pledge of the presence and action of the Holy Spirit in the faculties of the human being" (1813).

What a magnificent truth! God is within us. Through his grace, he dwells within our souls; he lives within our hearts. It's hard to wrap our minds around this remarkable truth—and that's why we ought to meditate on it continually and give thanks for it.

The Lord truly is with us—and in a way that is more intimate than we could imagine. Keeping this in mind and giving thanks for it helps us to avoid the sins mentioned above.

This truth can also change how we think about serious sin. When we think about serious sin (if we do at all!), we probably first think about its consequences more in relation to ourselves: separating us from God, endangering our souls, and so on. Important, for sure, but there's another side: if God dwells within us through grace, then mortal sin snuffs out the divine life within us. It turns the home of our hearts into a place that's cold, dark, unoccupied, and lonely. When we know the beauty, light, love, and warmth of the Lord's presence there, the reality of mortal sin is both sad and lonely.

But there is a solution! The sacrament of reconciliation, or penance. We are right around the midpoint of Advent, and it's a great time to think about going to confession, especially if we're aware of serious sin in our lives. A home is meant to be lived in, and if it's not, it grows cold, it gets dusty, and it becomes a shell of what it once was. Your heart is the home that you are readying for Christ at Christmas. Going to confession, even if you aren't aware of serious sin, is a beautiful way to prepare yourself for his arrival.

Joshua's conviction, "the LORD is with us," becomes "God with us" in the birth of Jesus, which we await (see Mt 1:23). Let us prepare our hearts for him to dwell there and for us to encounter him there in prayer. And one of the best ways to do this is through the sacrament of reconciliation. By confessing our sins, we receive the forgiveness and grace he wants to pour into our hearts.

Questions for Reflection and Discussion

- Of the sins against the theological virtues listed above, which one challenges you most? What would it take to overcome this?

- What keeps you from going to confession more often? What benefits come from going to confession regularly?

Resolutions to Consider

- Plan a time to go to confession this week.

- Start a novena for an increase in faith, hope, or love and a decrease in the sins against these.

- Remind yourself three times today that you can have confidence because the Lord is with you.

Build a Family Tradition

- With your family, read about or tell in your own words Joshua's role in Numbers 13–14 and Joshua 1.

- Help everyone to appreciate how Joshua brings to completion what Moses started. Note the main point: Joshua trusted mightily in the Lord's presence and in his help.

- Hang up your Jesse Tree ornament. (Suggested image: camel in the desert)

- Discuss the following: *If God is with us, the only thing we have to fear is sin. Why do we worry about so many other things?*

Day 14

Awaiting a King

The Story of Salvation: Judges 16:25–31 and 17:6

They called Samson out of the prison, and he made sport before them. They made him stand between the pillars; and Samson said to the lad who held him by the hand, "Let me feel the pillars on which the house rests, that I may lean against them." Now the house was full of men and women; all the lords of the Philis'tines were there, and on the roof there were about three thousand men and women, who looked on while Samson made sport.

Then Samson called to the LORD and said, "O Lord GOD, remember me, I beg you, and strengthen me, I beg you, only this once, O God, that I may be avenged upon the Philis'tines for one of my two eyes." And Samson grasped the two middle pillars upon which the house rested, and he leaned his weight upon them, his right hand on the one and his left hand on the other. And Samson said, "Let me die with the Philis'tines." Then he bowed with all his might; and the house fell upon the lords and upon all the people that were in it ... Then his brothers and all his family came down and took him and brought him up and buried him between Zorah and Esh'taol in the tomb of Mano'ah his father. He had judged Israel twenty years. ...

In those days there was no king in Israel; every man did what was right in his own eyes.

A Meditation for Today

Deep in my memory, I have a childhood image of Samson from a children's Bible. Samson is standing between two pillars, with his muscular arms outstretched, grasping the pillars with his huge hands and shaking them as the structure comes thundering down. And my reaction as a child: Samson is amazing!

But actually, Samson is very ... complicated. He is a judge, but he's also rough and impulsive; he has troubled relationships with women, and he has a tenuous relationship with God's law and with his own mission. So, he's complicated. And when I now read the book of Judges as an adult, I realize more and more that the whole book is like this: very complicated.

The book of Judges is like a pendulum swinging back and forth between sin and repentance, over and over again. It gets worse and worse, spiraling out of control until the tribes of Israel end up entangled in some of the most terrible sins and gruesome scenes in the entire Bible.

Okay, that went to a dark place pretty quickly. "Isn't Advent supposed to be a season of hope?" you're wondering. Yes, it is. But bear with me while I challenge that a little bit so that we can better understand what salvation is and the hope we have in it. Because here's the paradox: Christian hope presupposes a kind of hopelessness. And what I think the book of Judges captures, perhaps in greater detail than we would like, is the hopelessness of God's Chosen People in overcoming sin. The people fall into sin repeatedly; even the judges, who are meant to lead them back to the Lord, are flawed and can't rise above sin, as Samson demonstrates. The outlook is bleak.

Part of the problem seems to be that the people don't know where to look. Right after Samson, as things get worse and worse in the story, we are introduced to a kind of refrain that repeats in the final chapters of Judges: "*In those days, there was no king in Israel; every man did what was right in his own eyes.*" This line points ahead to Israel asking for a king, but it also acknowledges the need for God to be king and for him to rule over his people by ruling in their hearts. The people cannot rely only on themselves and their own strength.

A similar dynamic is still at work in our lives. The salvation Christ promises us is something so great that it exceeds our grasp; we cannot rely on ourselves and on our own strength to achieve it. And this is one of the main points that the *Catechism* makes when it discusses the theological virtue of hope: "Hope is the theological virtue by which we desire the kingdom of heaven and eternal life as our happiness, placing our trust in Christ's promises and relying not on our own strength, but on the help of the grace of the Holy Spirit" (1817). There are two basic movements within Christian hope. The first is not to rely on our own resources, because we realize they do not suffice for so great a good as salvation. The second is to rely instead on Christ, to trust in his promises, for he can bring about what goes beyond our powers.

A beautiful and very ordinary example of this can be seen in prayer. Prayer is essentially asking God for something. Now, I know that can sound a little uninspiring. It can sound like a matter of utility. You might even think it just sounds downright needy. But that's actually the point! To pray to the Lord and to ask him for something is to acknowledge that we can't do it on our own and that we need his help. It is to acknowledge the truth of who we are as needy and the truth of who he is as powerful and merciful.

The *Catechism*, in its section on prayer, expresses this in a helpful way: "By prayer of petition we express awareness of our relationship with God" (2629). Wow, from the simple idea of petition straight to the idea of relationship with God! It explains what it means: "We are creatures who are not our own beginning, not the masters of adversity, not our own last end. We are sinners who as Christians know that we have turned away from our Father. Our petition is already a turning back to him." How beautiful is that? Just by praying, we are turning back to God—we have to in order to address him. And when we address him and ask him for something, it shows our proper place before him as a beggar or, even better, as a child.

Are we aware of our own neediness? There's nowhere it becomes more evident than overcoming sin and attaining eternal life. The book of Judges makes very clear the impossibility of overcoming sin on our own, without God's help. And in Advent, we acknowledge this in a very specific way: we know we need Jesus Christ in order to be reconciled to the Father. Christ is in fact the solution, the help that the book of Judges cries out for! He is the King of Kings, who guides us with his law and his love so that *everyone does what is right in his eyes.*

And so we wait for him; we long for his coming at Christmas. For without him, we'd be lost and hopeless. That's a hard truth—but we have to own it to be ready to believe in the gospel, to hope in Christ's promise, and to love him for who he is and for the love he has for us.

Questions for Reflection and Discussion

- Do you realize your neediness when you pray? Or do you feel instead that God owes you his attention and gifts because of how good you are (at least compared to many other people) or what you've done? Humility is the first requirement of prayer; examine your heart and see whether your prayer acknowledges your need.

- What is the difference between the hopelessness that leads to Christian hope and total despair?

Resolutions to Consider

- Consider a sin you've struggled with for a while and give thanks, not for the sin itself, but for how this weakness manifests your need to rely on God.

- Perform one act today that requires you to humble yourself.

- Examine your conscience tonight with an emphasis on simplicity and humility.

Build a Family Tradition

- With your family, read or tell in your own words the story of Samson that reaches its high point in Judges 16.

- Point out the heroic and tragic elements of Samson's actions. Highlight the main idea: even the judges are very flawed leaders who make clear the need for a king, ultimately Christ.

- Hang up your Jesse Tree ornament. (Suggested image: broken pillar)

- Discuss the following: *What happens in a family if everyone does what is right in his own eyes?*

Day 15

Ordinary and Extraordinary

The Story of Salvation: Ruth 1:6, 8–11, and 13–17

Then [Na'omi] started with her daughters-in-law to return from the country of Moab, for she had heard in the country of Moab that the LORD had visited his people and given them food. . . . But [she] said to her two daughters-in-law, "Go, return each of you to her mother's house. May the LORD deal kindly with you, as you have dealt with the dead and with me. The LORD grant that you may find a home, each of you in the house of her husband!" Then she kissed them, and they lifted up their voices and wept. And they said to her, "No, we will return with you to your people." But Na'omi said, "Turn back, my daughters, why will you go with me? Have I yet sons in my womb that they may become your husbands? . . . No, my daughters, for it is exceedingly bitter to me for your sake that the hand of the LORD has gone forth against me." Then they lifted up their voices and wept again; and Orpah kissed her mother-in-law, but Ruth clung to her.

And she said, "See, your sister-in-law has gone back to her people and to her gods; return after your sister-in-law." But Ruth said, "Entreat me not to leave you or to return from following you; for where you go I will go, and where you lodge I will lodge; your people shall be my people, and your God my God; where you die I will die, and there will I be buried. May the LORD do so to me and more also if even death parts me from you."

A Meditation for Today

The book of Ruth is short, it's well-constructed, and it has a happy ending. It can remind us of an ordinary fairy tale. Naomi, Orpah, and Ruth find themselves in a tough spot after the death of their husbands. Naomi urges Orpah and Ruth to return to their homeland of Moab; Orpah she persuades, but Ruth stays by her side. Upon returning to Bethlehem, God's providence brings Ruth together with Boaz, a distant relative and wealthy landowner. They get married and they live happily ever after ... the end.

It's easy to be satisfied with it just so. But there are so many layers and depths of meaning at work—the book rewards a patient reading, and rereading!

Take Orpah, for example. Most of us have one of two reactions to her. The first is to just forget about her. This is very understandable; in fact, the book of Ruth sort of forgets about her: fourteen verses in, Orpah disappears from the text and into the shadows of history. The second reaction is to get a little judgy about Orpah. "How could she—leaving her mother-in-law behind?!" But really, she just obeys her mother-in-law, conceding her reasonable argument. Orpah resists at first, and only after continued persuasion does she leave in obedience and deference. It's very understandable, very natural, and very ordinary.

So, we're justified in kind of forgetting about Orpah, but not in judging her harshly. Why? Because Orpah represents the everyday, the normal, and even a certain kind of good. In a story that reads like an "ordinary fairy tale," she embodies the "ordinary."

But Ruth? Well, Ruth is extraordinary. She reminds us that even in the midst of ordinary fairy tales and ordinary circumstances, we can find extraordinary heroes. Her clinging to Naomi and, most amazing of all, coming to share Naomi's faith in the one true God of Israel are extraordinary by any measure. In fact, both Ruth and Boaz are presented as extraordinary heroes in the midst of ordinary life. The text introduces Boaz as a "mighty man of valor" in the first verse of chapter two. This designation has heroic overtones as it refers both backward to the judges and forward to King David. But Boaz manifests his greatness in the ordinary: having the name of the Lord on his lips, showing generous hospitality and care toward Ruth and Naomi, and taking Ruth as his wife in a way that meets, and even exceeds, the requirements of the law and of righteousness.

And, like a match made in heaven, Ruth is also later called a "woman of valor" (Ruth 3:11). Both of these characters show their worth in virtue and that they are fitting partners: two ordinary people, heroic in virtue, brought together by God's providence.

The best and most important example of their extraordinary character is how they reflect God's loving kindness. This is a particular kind of love, typically said of God, that in Hebrew is called *hesed*. It is a faithful, generous, steadfast, and merciful love. Both Ruth and Boaz demonstrate this kind of love toward each other and, by doing this, they give us a depiction of how the love between man and woman, especially in marriage, is meant to reflect God's love for us. In this way, the ordinary reality of marriage—with its ups and downs, its joys and challenges—is elevated to extraordinary heights. It becomes the place where extraordinary love is meant to be present and to be a sign of God's own love.

Which points to the larger truth: in the Christian world and imagination, there is nothing so ordinary that it cannot be elevated to extraordinary heights through charity. Whether we are married or not, it is the measure of our love that will lift us into the realm of the extraordinary or limit us to the ordinary.

Let me mention one last point or layer in this story: we share in these truths not only because we are connected to Ruth and Boaz by our humanity, but also because we are connected to them by genealogy. The book takes genealogies seriously, opening and closing with them. And the one that closes the book presents to us for the first time the name "Jesse." Yes, that Jesse ... the Jesse for which the Jesse Tree originated," perhaps?

No, actually, this Jesse *is* the Jesse of the Jesse Tree, but he's made famous by his son, David, and it is to David that the final genealogy in Ruth points. Why David? David will be the king who restores the people from the terrible sins of the period of the judges—and David's line will be the line in which Jesus will take his place as the ultimate and rightful king, not only of the Jewish people, not only of the world, but of the universe. We are grafted into Christ and thus also share in his genealogy. The *Catechism* explains: "Christ enables us *to live in him* all that he himself lived, and *he lives it in us.* . . . We are called only to become one with him, for he enables us as the members of his Body to share in what he lived for us in his flesh as our model" (521). We live in Christ all that he lived, including being a descendant of King David. And so the genealogy at the end of Ruth points not only to Jesus but also to us.

In other words, we're drawn into the book of Ruth not only by the invitation it makes to find the extraordinary in the ordinary but also by the way it points ahead to Jesse, to King David, to Jesus, and, through him, to us.

Questions for Reflection and Discussion

- For those of us who are married and have families, we should ask ourselves: how do I love my spouse and children? Would others see in our interactions a reflection of God's own love? What are one or two areas where I can do better, where I can love better?

- For those who are not married, whether single or religious, the same kinds of questions apply: how do I love my friends, those with whom I interact each day? How could I improve to better reflect the love that Christ demonstrated for us?

Resolutions to Consider

- Find one ordinary act today that you can do with extraordinary love, making it heroic.

- Some acts of love become merely like a duty or routine. Perform one of these with attention and delight this week.

Build a Family Tradition

- With your family, read or tell in your own words the story of Ruth.

- Notice how Ruth and Boaz care for each other, others, and God in word and deed. Emphasize the main point: Ruth and Boaz pave the way for King David and ultimately, for Christ.

- Hang up your Jesse Tree ornament. (Suggested image: sheaf of wheat)

- Discuss the following: *Can you think of a time when love made an ordinary day or moment into something really special and extraordinary?*

Day 16

David's Temple

The Story of Salvation: 2 Samuel 7:1–13

Now when the king dwelt in his house, and the LORD had given him rest from all his enemies round about, the king said to Nathan the prophet, "See now, I dwell in a house of cedar, but the ark of God dwells in a tent." And Nathan said to the king, "Go, do all that is in your heart; for the LORD is with you."

But that same night the word of the LORD came to Nathan, "Go and tell my servant David, 'Thus says the LORD: Would you build me a house to dwell in? I have not dwelt in a house since the day I brought up the sons of Israel from Egypt to this day, but I have been moving about in a tent for my dwelling. … Did I speak a word with any of the judges of Israel, whom I commanded to shepherd my people Israel, saying, "Why have you not built me a house of cedar?"'… 'Thus says the LORD of hosts, I took you from the pasture, from following the sheep, that you should be prince over my people Israel; and I have been with you wherever you went, and have cut off all your enemies from before you; and I will make for you a great name, like the name of the great ones of the earth. And I will appoint a place for my people Israel, and will plant them, that they may dwell in their own place, and be disturbed no more; and violent men shall afflict them no more, as formerly, from the time that I appointed judges over my people Israel; and I will give you rest from all your enemies. Moreover, the LORD declares to you that the LORD will make you a house. When your days are fulfilled and you lie down with your fathers, I will raise up your offspring after you, who shall come forth from your body, and I will establish his kingdom. He shall build a house for my name, and I will establish the throne of his kingdom forever.'"

A Meditation for Today

Great-hearted David wants to build a temple for God to dwell in. What better thing could he want to do? What greater gift or purer motivation could we imagine? Naturally, God will be thrilled by this gift, but still, humble-hearted David runs it by Nathan, the prophet, who gives implicit approval: "Go, do all that is in your heart." But then God shows up, and instead of being flattered and delighted by this gift idea, he basically says, "No. It's not on my gift registry. I never asked for that. It's not what I want."

Ouch.

I think there's a great lesson here for trying to discern and follow God's will. Our ideas, as good as they may be, are not always God's ideas. God doesn't always ask the biggest and best of us. He doesn't always want the newest and shiniest thing from us. Now, of course, sometimes he does, and that's what can make discernment tricky—and also exciting. But the basic point is just because we have a good idea, even a great idea, doesn't mean it's God's idea. It doesn't do away with our need to spend time with God in prayer and to ask him to make his will known to us. We always have to ask him to lead and guide us, to give us clarity of vision and then the fortitude of heart to follow it.

It's not easy when we have a great idea and God says, "No" or "Not right now," whether in prayer or in the events that befall us. I don't think David found it easy either. But David's story does provide us with some consolation: God's plans are better than ours.

In Advent, it's worthwhile to take notice of the way God generously inverts David's proposal: you won't build me a house, but I will build you a house and an everlasting kingdom. This kingdom is fulfilled in Christ, who ushers in the kingdom of God and who reigns as the King of Kings. But I want to highlight another way that God's plans are better than David's, a way that David does actually get to give God a gift that's better than the temple he had in mind.

David didn't get to construct that temple built of stone; he didn't get to consecrate a place as holy. But he did give God a temple built of words—consecrating time as holy and making holy the heart that prays those words in time. David gave God the Psalms.

Many of the Psalms are explicitly attributed to King David and, taken all together, the book of Psalms is "the masterwork of prayer in the Old Testament"—that's how the *Catechism* describes it (2585). It also links David's prayers to his being a man after God's own heart. It says, "David is par excellence the king 'after God's own heart,' the shepherd who prays for his people and prays in their name. His submission to the will of God, his praise, and his repentance will be a model for the prayer of the people. … In the Psalms David, inspired by the Holy Spirit, is the first prophet of Jewish and Christian prayer" (2579). The Psalms are an enduring and essential element in the life of the Church and in the lives of believers because they are prayed by Christ and fulfilled in him, too. There's something in the Psalms for every time and occasion, and for this reason, the Church, in her Liturgy of the Hours, prays the Psalms every day, throughout the day.

We do well to pray the Psalms also, even to memorize them. Start with Psalm 1; it's short and beautiful and profound. Or pick another psalm, at random or an old favorite. Maybe pay special attention to the psalm at Mass. The main thing is just to pray the Psalms. When we do, we find timeless and fruitful lessons in how to pray: with trust, in praise, with honest and straightforward hearts, and with the humility to ask God for the things we truly need.

More than a temple of stone, this is what God wants: a temple in time and in our hearts; a temple in our minds and meditations; a temple of prayer. More important than anything we can do or make or accomplish is simply our relationship with God in prayer and the time we spend together. This is the secret to David being a man after God's own heart.

And, you know what, it's actually not a secret! We too can be men and women after God's own heart, by having David's heart, a heart of prayer, and a temple of words spoken to God in time.

Questions for Reflection and Discussion

- Can you think of a time when things didn't go according to your plan but turned out better than you expected or hoped? How can these moments be sources of light and hope for us when our plans don't seem to be working out?

- How do you discern whether God is calling you to persevere when things aren't going as planned or to let your plans go in order to embrace his?

Resolutions to Consider

- Plan to pray a psalm (consider Psalm 4, 23, or 121) before going to bed.

- Commit to paying extra attention to the psalm at Mass and to praying along.

- Give a word of encouragement to someone you know who is discerning God's will amid an unexpected situation.

Build a Family Tradition

- With your family, read or tell in your own words the story of David wanting to build a temple in 2 Samuel 7.

- Appreciate together how noble David's aspiration seems. Note the main point: God inverts David's hope and offers him something even better.

- Hang up your Jesse Tree ornament. (Suggested image: Star of David)

- Discuss the following: *What can help us to trust in God's plan for us, even when it isn't what we expect?*

Day 17

Conversion Is More Than a Moment

The Story of Salvation: Psalm 51:1–12

Have mercy on me, O God,
*   according to your merciful love;*
*   according to your abundant mercy*
blot out my transgressions.
Wash me thoroughly from my iniquity,
*   and cleanse me from my sin!*

For I know my transgressions,
*   and my sin is ever before me.*
Against you, you only, have I sinned,
*   and done that which is evil in your sight,*
so that you are justified in your sentence
*   and blameless in your judgment.*

Behold, I was brought forth in iniquity,
and in sin did my mother conceive me.

Behold, you desire truth in the inward being;
therefore teach me wisdom in my secret heart.
Purge me with hyssop, and I shall be clean;
wash me, and I shall be whiter than snow.
Let me hear joy and gladness;
let the bones which you have broken rejoice.
Hide your face from my sins,
and blot out all my iniquities.

Create in me a clean heart, O God,
and put a new and right spirit within me.
Cast me not away from your presence,
and take not your holy Spirit from me.
Restore to me the joy of your salvation,
and uphold me with a willing spirit.

A Meditation for Today

King David is a "man after [God's] own heart" (1 Sam 13:14). He's an obedient son. He's a courageous warrior. He's a loyal subject, acting with justice and piety toward Saul, his wayward predecessor. He's a strong king, a unifying leader. And yet, what we've heard today is a psalm of David that reveals the depths of a heart that is humbly contrite and very much in need of mercy.

But wait a minute: Which is it? Is David a man after God's own heart—which needless to say is without sin? Or is he a sinner in need of mercy?

The beginning of our psalm actually gives us an answer: the preface identifies it as a psalm of David, written after Nathan, the prophet, confronted David about his adultery with Bathsheba. So, there's no doubt that David is a sinner in need of mercy. The bones of his righteousness have been broken by sin, and only when bound up by mercy can healing and rejoicing follow.

But knowing this about the psalm might make it easy to pass over its words too quickly. We might think that they only express the kind of sorrow and need for mercy we would have after some major failure. But it captures a lot more than this.

One way we know this is by looking at how frequently the psalm enters into the Liturgy of the Hours, the prayer of the Church—it's present every day, not in its entirety, but in part. The first words prayed in the morning at the start of the Liturgy of the Hours are taken from Psalm 51: "Lord, open my lips, and my mouth will proclaim your praise" (Ps 51:15). This continual repetition and calling to mind of David's psalm brings home the point that conversion of heart is more than a moment. It's more than reaching rock bottom and turning to God. It's more than falling into serious sin and returning to the Lord.

It *is* these things, but it goes beyond these moments, too. Conversion is an ongoing and ever-present part of the Christian's life. The *Catechism* quotes from Psalm 51 in a few places, but one of them speaks directly about conversion. First, the *Catechism* talks about Jesus' call to conversion and what can be called the "first and fundamental conversion": the turning to Christ that happens at the beginning of the Christian life through faith and baptism (1427). It then goes on to describe another meaning of conversion, and this is where Psalm 51 appears: "Christ's call to conversion continues to resound in the lives of Christians. This *second conversion* is an uninterrupted task for the whole Church who, 'clasping sinners to her bosom, [is] at once holy and always in need of purification, [and] follows constantly the path of penance and renewal.' This endeavor of conversion is not just a human work. It is the movement of a 'contrite heart,' drawn and moved by grace to respond to the merciful love of God who loved us first" (1428).

So, the whole of the Christian life is a work of conversion—of turning to the Lord more and more, over and over again, and receiving his mercy. When we do this, we grow in intimacy with him. This might sound like a lot of work and a long process. It often is. But it's also an exciting prospect. The Lord is only beginning his work in you. He has so much in store for you. He wants to transform you from head to toe, to increase his love in your heart more than you can imagine. This is ongoing conversion and it's nothing other than the exciting path and adventure of Christian discipleship, learning from the Master and imitating him.

What does this look like concretely? Well, it doesn't have to look like falling into serious sin, as King David did. If it does, then the sacrament of reconciliation is the way to go—and what a beautiful encounter with mercy it is! But much more often, conversion doesn't look like David's "big mistake". It looks less like a serious sin followed by confession and more like small sins followed by a heartfelt act of contrition—which could even be by praying this psalm! Even apart from sin, it looks very simply like turning to the Lord and giving our hearts to him ... again and again.

Another place in our lives where this conversion happens in a small but beautiful way is whenever we pray. When we look to the Church's spiritual tradition, a common counsel is to begin prayer by confessing our neediness and sin and turning once again to God to seek his mercy. After all, prayer is coming to the Divine Physician, bringing our broken bones to him so that he can enfold them in his mercy and restore them. Prayer is coming before God to talk with him, to place our needs before him. And in prayer one of our first needs is for his help to pray well, and this begins by purifying our hearts so that they're ready to love him, to receive him, to rejoice with him.

Concretely, this looks like beginning prayer by turning our thoughts and heart toward the Lord, which means also turning away from ourselves, our self-love, our sin, and our weakness. We begin prayer by placing ourselves in the presence of the Lord, remembering how close he is to us, and then turning toward him by confessing our sins, asking for forgiveness, and giving our hearts to him once again. It only takes a few moments ... and then we can carry on with prayer as usual. Only I think you won't find it to be quite the same as usual, since this small beginning can renew our prayer considerably when we really commit ourselves to it.

Advent itself is a time of conversion: of turning toward Christ. It's an opportunity, a time for conversion in our own hearts. Psalm 51, in particular, not only reminds us of that but it can help us do just that.

In this way, it also reminds us that the Psalms are an ever-ready source and guide for prayer, in this case preparing our hearts to welcome Christ this Christmas.

Questions for Reflection and Discussion

- Do you usually think of discipleship as involving ongoing conversion? Why or why not?

- Do you have a favorite saint who exemplifies this ongoing process of turning to the Lord more and more, over and over?

Resolutions to Consider

- Plan to begin your prayer time this week with a short moment of conversion, turning toward the Lord, turning away from self-love, and placing yourself in his presence.

- Consciously turn your heart toward the Lord three times today or tomorrow: morning, midday, and evening.

- If you've fallen into serious sin, plan to go to confession this week.

Build a Family Tradition

- Read Psalm 51 with your family, reminding them prior to this reading about the story of David and Bathsheba and recalling the big sin that King David committed prior to this reading.

- Note the main point of the psalm: King David has to ask God's forgiveness after a big mistake and we do too.

- Hang up your Jesse Tree ornament. (Suggested image: a clean heart)

- Discuss the following: *Why is it important for a follower of Christ to turn toward him and return to him again and again?*

Day 18

An Undivided Heart

The Story of Salvation: 1 Kings 3:5–7, 9–14

At Gib'eon the LORD appeared to Solomon in a dream by night; and God said, "Ask what I shall give you." And Solomon said, "You have shown great and steadfast love to your servant David my father, because he walked before you in faithfulness, in righteousness, and in uprightness of heart toward you; and you have kept for him this great and merciful love ... And now, O LORD my God, you have made your servant king in place of David my father, although I am but a little child; ... Give your servant therefore an understanding mind to govern your people, that I may discern between good and evil; for who is able to govern this great people of yours?"

It pleased the LORD that Solomon had asked this. And God said to him, "Because you have asked this, and have not asked for yourself long life or riches or the life of your enemies, but have asked for

> *yourself understanding to discern what is right, behold, I now do*
> *according to your word. Behold, I give you a wise and discerning*
> *mind, so that none like you has been before you and none like you*
> *shall arise after you. I give you also what you have not asked, both*
> *riches and honor, so that no other king shall compare with you, all*
> *your days. And if you will walk in my ways, keeping my statutes*
> *and my commandments, as your father David walked, then I will*
> *lengthen your days."*

A Meditation for Today

We all have many desires of different sorts and of varying degrees of importance. So, what a clarifying question it would be to have God ask us directly: "What would you have me give to you?" How would we respond? How would *you* respond?

Solomon is given the chance to answer this clarifying question, and he answers well: he asks for wisdom, especially so that he might rule well.

This moment calls to mind multiple scenes we've already considered in our reflections on the Jesse Tree this Advent. Solomon wants to know good and evil, in order to govern the people well. But unlike Adam and Eve *grasping* for this knowledge themselves, Solomon asks for the wisdom to discern between good and evil, to *receive* this knowledge as God has established it. He doesn't ask for long life, which includes well-being, comfort, and pleasure, all of which tempted Abraham, Isaac, and Jacob in various ways. He doesn't ask for riches or fame, at least the latter tempting the people at Babel. Nor does he ask for the life of his enemies, a kind of power over them, as Cain demonstrated so clearly in his pursuit of power through killing and through establishing a city.

How is it that Solomon is able to avoid these temptations and ask for what is truly essential and glorifying to God? He has an undivided heart. To attain wisdom, our hearts must be undivided. Our loves have to be well ordered so that we love the most important things most, and the least important things, well, least—and we love them *for the sake of* the most important things. Solomon shows us the unity and order of an undivided heart, wishing for true wisdom so that his power over the people as king will serve them and guide them according to God's holy will.

It's truly a beautiful scene, but alas, it doesn't last long. The end of 1 Kings tells of Solomon's undivided heart becoming divided: it goes after all the things he didn't ask for originally. Splintered between these disordered loves, Solomon's vision becomes clouded, and his judgment suffers. Then, unable to exercise kingly power in an upright and wise way, his reign goes downhill.

We are awaiting Christ's coming at Christmas, and with his coming, we find once again, and even more so, that perfect harmony of a unified heart and its pursuit of wisdom for the sake of governing well. St. Paul calls Christ "the power of God and the wisdom of God" in 1 Corinthians 1:24. And these two terms remind us of Solomon, who asked for wisdom to exercise his power well. We're reminded of both his greatness and his downfall. Both of these point in different ways to Christ. He is the wisdom of God incarnate, referring back to and bringing to perfection Solomon's greatness. But he also stands strong where Solomon fell;

he remains perfectly wise and undivided in the face of temptation, for example, when Satan leads him out into the desert and offers him the same kinds of things that made Solomon's heart go astray.

Given this contrast, we likely wonder how to discover whether our heart is divided and what the loves are that sometimes secretly compete with love for God and his wisdom. One of the best ways to measure how undivided our hearts are is to consider our distractions in prayer. Prayer is meant to be time for God, but our other wishes and loves often creep in and overshadow our first love, our love for God. This happens to all of us and it isn't a reason to lose heart. The *Catechism* offers some wise and consoling words about distraction in prayer: "To set about hunting down distractions would be to fall into their trap, when all that is necessary is to turn back to our heart: for a distraction reveals to us what we are attached to, and this humble awareness before the Lord should awaken our preferential love for him and lead us resolutely to offer him our heart to be purified" (2729). Becoming aware of our distractions in prayer can be a moment of great grace, showing us where our treasure, and therefore our hearts, truly lie (see Mt 6:21). Then we just give these desires and our hearts back to God, asking for his grace to put first things first and then to let all the other things follow that.

After all, this is what God promised to Solomon and what Christ promises us as well: when we put God and his kingdom first, then all the other goods are also given to us—but in a unified way rather than in a way that divides our hearts, splinters our attention, and disorders our loves. The reward for *undivided* hearts is *unified* riches: wisdom, grace, eternal life, and then also the material things and comforts and pleasures we need for the vocation that God has given us, but all in the right order.

We might wish for a direct and clarifying question like Solomon received. But here's the thing: God gives himself to us each day, in prayer and, in a special way, in the holy Eucharist. And by putting himself out there like that, God does indirectly ask us what we would like from him today. How do we answer? There are so many good things in the world, but do we have undivided hearts to ask for the most important thing? We should be grateful for the gift we are able to receive of the Lord's intimate presence; and we should be grateful to learn how our hearts wander, preferring other things, for only then can we ask the Lord to lead them back to him and to make them undivided in pursuit of him and his wisdom.

Questions for Reflection and Discussion

- What is your heart like right now? What are your loves like? Are you more like the young, undivided Solomon or the old, divided Solomon?

- Which of the many good things that God gives us do we tend to prefer: good work, good friends, good food, good times? When do we sometimes prefer these to God, wisdom, or prayer?

Resolutions to Consider

- Decide to go to Mass this week when you might not typically go, putting God first in a concrete way.

- Pay close attention this week to the distractions that arise during your prayer and what they reveal about your loves.

- Ask God to give you the gift of wisdom.

Build a Family Tradition

- With your family, read or tell in your own words the beginning of Solomon's kingship in 1 Kings 3.

- Note the importance of the question God asks and then marvel at Solomon's remarkable answer.

- Hang up your Jesse Tree ornament. (Suggested image: scales of justice)

- Discuss the following: *How do you think you might have answered the question God asked Solomon?*

Day 19

Hearing the Whisper

The Story of Salvation: 1 Kings 19:4–13

[Eli'jah] went a day's journey into the wilderness, and came and sat down under a broom tree; and he asked that he might die, saying, "It is enough; now, O LORD, take away my life; for I am no better than my fathers." And he lay down and slept under a broom tree; and behold, an angel touched him, "Arise and eat." And he looked, and behold, there was at his head a cake baked on hot stones and a jar of water. And he ate and drank, and lay down again. And the angel of the LORD came again a second time, and touched him, and said, "Arise and eat, else the journey will be too great for you." And he arose, and ate and drank, and walked in the strength of that food forty days and forty nights to Horeb the mount of God.

And there he came to a cave, and lodged there; and behold, the word of the LORD came to him, and he said to him, "What are

you doing here, Eli'jah?" He said, "I have been very jealous for
the LORD, the God of hosts; for the sons of Israel have forsaken
your covenant, thrown down your altars, and slain your prophets
with the sword; and I, even I only, am left; and they seek my life,
to take it away." And he said, "Go forth, and stand upon the
mount before the LORD." And behold, the LORD passed by, and
a great and strong wind tore the mountains, and broke in pieces
the rocks before the LORD, but the LORD was not in the wind;
and after the wind an earthquake, but the LORD was not in the
earthquake; and after the earthquake a fire, but the LORD was
not in the fire; and after the fire a still small voice. And when
Eli'jah heard it, he wrapped his face in his mantle and went out
and stood at the entrance of the cave.

A Meditation for Today

Elijah—he steps onto the Old Testament scene all of a sudden. After
the death of Solomon, God's Chosen People are plagued once again
with ups and downs, divisions, a series of bad kings, and a struggle to
be faithful to the covenant. And in the midst of this, Elijah appears in
1 Kings chapter 17 as a prophet of the Lord. He confronts King Ahab
in Israel. He announces a drought as punishment for the evil done by
the king. Then he stays with the widow of Zarephath, who feeds him
generously using flour from a jar and oil from a jug that miraculously
never run out. When the widow's son falls ill and dies, Elijah brings
him back from the dead. As though that weren't impressive enough,
Elijah then throws down the gauntlet and challenges the prophets of

Baal, a false god, in a dramatic contest between their god and his God. Of course, since the God of Israel is the only real God, he wins! Elijah calls down fire from heaven, sent by the only true God, the God of Abraham, Isaac, and Jacob, and it consumes the sacrifice in a display of might and power.

It's after these stunning feats, at the height of his accomplishments—the zenith of Elijah's career, really—that a funny thing happens. Elijah hears that King Ahab's wife, the evil Jezebel, seeks to have him killed. He fears for his life. He flees. And next thing we know, we have the scene above: he's under a broom tree in the wilderness, asking the Lord to just let him die. What ... an ... emotional rollercoaster!

So, what can we learn from this scene?

Beyond the fact that Elijah seems to have a hankering for cake, one of the lessons here is that Elijah has to listen to the Lord's voice in order to learn what the Lord wants him to do—following God's will is paramount, but this requires listening, hearing his voice. And God doesn't always—in fact, doesn't often—speak in ways that are loud and dramatic. Elijah hears God's voice not in the wind, not in the earthquake, not in the fire—none of these obvious, dramatic events convey God's voice. Instead, God speaks in the sound of a low whisper. It's something quiet, something small, something that could easily be missed. God doesn't knock Elijah upside the head with his will. He invites him to listen carefully and closely and to find him in a quiet, little whisper. God's ways are humble ways.

We, too, have to listen for the Lord's voice. Why? Because we are called to holiness, and holiness is simply doing God's will. The *Catechism* underscores this point when talking about Christian holiness: "'All Christians in any state or walk of life are called to the fullness of Christian life and to the perfection of charity.' All are called to holiness ... 'In order to reach this perfection the faithful should use the strength dealt out to them by Christ's gift, so that ... doing the will of the Father in everything, they may wholeheartedly devote themselves to the glory of God and to the service of their neighbor'" (2013). So, if we are to do the will of God in everything, where do we find it? How do we hear it?

Saint Teresa of Avila said we hear God in his providence: in an event, in a homily that we hear, in a friend's comment or correction, in a challenge that confronts us, in a scriptural passage we read, and on and on. The point is that we don't usually hear his voice in a big, obvious way. God is not limited to our human mode of speech. He speaks in a way appropriate to God—by arranging the universe and its events in such a way that manifests his will to us. But we have to have eyes to see and ears to hear. We have to look and listen attentively, quieting our own hearts and quelling our own distractions so that we can become aware of how God is speaking to us in and through his providence.

How can we become more aware of God's voice? How can we hear his voice more regularly so that we can do his will? A great place to start is by realizing that he's always speaking. And so, finding God's will, hearing his voice, begins by growing in trust: trusting that everything that happens is a part of God's providence. He is in control, and not only in a big cosmic way but also in a way where he is arranging things for your own good. He is speaking to *you* in the events, and words, and sentiments of each day. He wills each thing and each moment for *your* good. And he offers you the grace in each moment to live up to whatever you face. What about the bad things? He allows those, too, but only for a greater good.

Be convinced, remind yourself constantly, that each moment of your life is a gift of God's providence. Let's look for God in his gentle providence. Let's *listen* for the whisper. Advent is the perfect time for this because what we're waiting for is a whisper of sorts: in the midst of the grand Roman Empire and the noise of Roman rule, Jesus enters the world in a humble and quiet way. It's like a whisper, heard only by those who are listening.

Questions for Reflection and Discussion

- Why doesn't God speak loudly or powerfully more often? What does his whisper ask of us?

- What are the most prominent obstacles or distractions that prevent you from hearing the quiet whisper of God's voice?

Resolutions to Consider

- Start forming a habit of seeing and trusting in God's providence; remind yourself regularly that God is in control.

- Spend more time listening in prayer.

- Reduce the amount of noise and distraction in your life.

Build a Family Tradition

- With your family, read or tell in your own words the story of Elijah in 1 Kings 17–19.

- Note the powerful deeds that Elijah does, but then how he also swings to fear for his life. Highlight the importance of Elijah listening for God's voice.

- Hang up your Jesse Tree ornament. (Suggested image: a cave)

- Discuss the following: *What things in our life can make it hard to hear the whisper of God's voice?*

Day 20

The Jesse Stump

The Story of Salvation: Isaiah 11:1–6

There shall come forth a shoot from the stump of Jesse,
and a branch shall grow out of his roots.
And the Spirit of the LORD shall rest upon him,
the spirit of wisdom and understanding,
the spirit of counsel and might,
the spirit of knowledge and the fear of the LORD.
And his delight shall be in the fear of the LORD.

He shall not judge by what his eyes see,
or decide by what his ears hear;
but with righteousness he shall judge the poor,
and decide with equity for the meek of the earth;
and he shall strike the earth with the rod of his mouth,
and with the breath of his lips he shall slay the wicked.
Righteousness shall be the belt of his waist,
and faithfulness the belt of his loins.

The wolf shall dwell with the lamb,
and the leopard shall lie down with the kid,
and the calf and the lion and the fatling together,
and a little child shall lead them.

A Meditation for Today

We finally arrive at the main biblical text from which we get the idea of the Jesse Tree: from the stump of Jesse, a shoot comes forth, and from his roots, a branch! It's all right there: a tree sprouting up from Jesse!

But it's a slightly odd image of the Jesse Tree, and it raises three questions for us.

First, we notice that it's a chopped-down tree, just a "stump", that, along with its roots, refuses to give up and puts out a meager little shoot. So, first question: Why isn't this a normal tree?

Well, it's clear that the image being used is like a family tree. And Jesse's son, David, established the kingdom of Israel. But after David's reign, the kingdom was first divided and then conquered. So, the trunk that continued up from the stump of Jesse was cut off. But God promised David an everlasting kingdom, and he is faithful to his promises. Only later will a shoot come forth to restore the Davidic kingship, ultimately in Christ, who is in the line of David and the everlasting king.

The second question we might ask about this odd tree has to do with what's below the stump: the roots, we could say. We first saw the name "Jesse" in the book of Ruth. He's Ruth's grandchild and the father of

King David. But what we didn't focus on in the Book of Ruth is something quite remarkable. God's people are set apart from the nations and because of this, intermarriage with other nations is typically frowned upon and, in some cases, forbidden. This is what makes it remarkable that both Ruth and Boaz have roots outside the Jewish people. Ruth is a Moabite, and Boaz is a descendant of Judah and Tamar, a Canaanite. And *that* is what makes this tree of Jesse not a purebred, heirloom variety tree but a hybrid. So, that's our second question: Why is it a hybrid?

Well, the first thing to say is, thank God it's a hybrid! Because that is what enables most of us to have a place in it. Most Catholics, most Christians, are not of Jewish descent but instead are Gentiles brought into the fold through Christ. God's plan was always to incorporate the nations, but how he would do that remained a mystery. The inclusion of other nations in the family line springing from Ruth and Boaz, and therefore in the tree of Jesse, hints at the future "catholic" People of God, one that embraces all nations.

All of this leads us to our third question: Can such a chopped-down, branch-sprouting, hybrid tree produce fruit? Yes, and of the finest quality! There is a sense in which Christ can be said to be the branch and the fruit: he is the messianic fulfillment of the prophecy, the Son of God become man, and the first fruit in which we all share. But, in another sense, if Christ is the branch, then we are the fruit that it bears: through our baptism into Christ, we bear the fruit of his grace, of eternal life within us, the very finest fruit we could imagine. In fact, today's passage mentions some of the best fruit that faith bears in our lives: the gifts of the Holy Spirit. These gifts—wisdom, understanding, knowledge, counsel, fortitude, reverence, fear of the Lord—make us docile to the Holy Spirit, pliable in the Lord's hands, so that the fruit we bear will be abundant.

What lessons can we draw from a tree that doesn't grow straight, isn't a purebred, and doesn't appear to bear fruit? We learn that God doesn't draw his plans in straight lines; that his plan of salvation is meant for all, it's catholic; and that he wants this tree and this plan to bear fruit in our lives.

Christ is the messianic fulfillment of this prophecy about the tree of Jesse. We are grafted into him; we are members of his Body. And so this genealogy, this tree, is ours too! We've talked previously about this genealogy, but this is going a step further to see that the Jesse Tree is not just a devotion we do to get in touch with a distant but important past. *It's a way of returning to and rediscovering our family tree, our family history, and finding out what that history means for us.*

We can do this because, as the *Catechism* teaches, the " 'family of God' is gradually formed and takes shape during the stages of human history, in keeping with the Father's plan. In fact, 'already present in figure at the beginning of the world, this Church was prepared in marvelous fashion in the history of the people of Israel' " (759). The Church is the family of God; it's our family. And, like any family, we have a family tree that prepared the way for us. But unlike other family trees, ours has a name: Jesse. Our family tree in Christ is the Jesse Tree.

Back at the *very* beginning, we said the Jesse Tree is a devotional practice of running through the major figures and events of salvation history. But now I hope we see clearly that it's more than just that—it's not like we're just reading an account of the history of God's people. Instead, we've seen that it is our history, too. First, in the way that these situations confront us still today, and thus the temptations and triumphs are present in our lives as well. But second, it's our history because, for those of us who are members of Christ's Body, we share in his genealogy, which traces its way back through David, Jesse, Obed, Ruth, and even further back through Judah, Jacob, Isaac, Abraham, and ultimately, Adam.

In Advent, it's truly a gift to follow the tradition of the Jesse Tree. It allows us to return to Scripture, not simply as a Bible study to grow in familiarity with a text, but to return to our roots, rediscover our family line, and find our story within the story of Scripture.

So, take a moment today—and each day for the rest of Advent—to marvel at our family tree and perhaps to reflect again on which character or story reflects where you are right now—your strengths, your weaknesses, your challenges, your questions. God is near us. He's always speaking to us. And the chances are high that he wants to speak to you through the characters and stories of the Jesse Tree.

Questions for Reflection and Discussion

- How important to you is your family tree? What does it mean to you to be grafted into the remarkable family tree that is the Jesse Tree?

- Is there a particular scriptural figure or moment that has resonated with you thus far? Why might that be, and what might you learn from it?

Resolutions to Consider

- Pick one instance in your life that God seemed to be writing with crooked lines; remind yourself that he brings amazing things out of imperfect stories.

- Choose a figure we've considered in these Jesse Tree reflections and commit to keeping him or her in mind this week as someone to learn from.

- Set aside some time to reflect on how the Lord brought it about that you became grafted into this remarkable family tree through Christ.

Build a Family Tradition

- With your family, read or tell in your own words the prophecy of Isaiah in Isaiah 11.

- Note the image of the stump of Jesse and the living shoot that emerges from it. Mention how this points ahead to both King David and Jesus Christ.

- Hang up your Jesse Tree ornament. (Suggested image: tree stump with sprouting shoot)

- Discuss the following: *Why doesn't God use the image of a tall, noble oak tree instead of a short stump?*

Day 21

Written on the Heart

The Story of Salvation: Jeremiah 31:31–36

"Behold, the days are coming, says the LORD, when I will make a new covenant with the house of Israel and the house of Judah, not like the covenant which I made with their fathers when I took them by the hand to bring them out of the land of Egypt, my covenant which they broke, and I showed myself their Master, says the LORD. But this is the covenant which I will make with the house of Israel after those days, says the LORD: I will put my law within them, and I will write it upon their hearts; and I will be their God, and they shall be my people. And no longer shall each one teach his neighbor and each his brother, saying, 'Know the LORD,' for they shall all know me, from the least of them to the greatest, says the LORD; for I will forgive their iniquity, and I will remember their sin no more."

Thus says the LORD,
who gives the sun for light by day
*   and the fixed order of the moon and the stars for light by night,*
who stirs up the sea so that its waves roar—
*   the LORD of hosts is his name:*
"If this fixed order departs
*   from before me, says the LORD,*
then shall the offspring of Israel cease
*   from being a nation before me forever."*

A Meditation for Today

Ever since Adam and Eve gave in to the serpent's temptation, there has been a division running through the heart of the human person. The consequences of that first sin reveal to us the depth and reach of this division: Adam and Eve experience shame at their nakedness, a division between body and soul; they hide from God in the garden, a division between humans and God; they experience increased strife in their relationship, a division between man and woman; they experience toil in their labor, a division between humans and the earth. From the individual to society to the earth, division abounds.

As we've walked through the stories and figures of salvation history, we've seen these divisions playing out in various ways. But this prophecy of Jeremiah refers to one of the largest effects and signs of the division that sin brought into the world: the divided houses or kingdoms of the Jewish people—the house of Israel and the house of Judah, as our reading puts it.

Although the consequences are dire and on display, at this point, the prophet sounds a hopeful message. Jeremiah emphasizes not the division but rather the *healing* of this division, the unification of the divided kingdoms of Israel and Judah. When God ushers in a new covenant with his people, it will restore unity, bringing about the one people of God. Healing this large-scale social division begins with where the division began in the first place: in the human heart. And thus, God speaks beautifully of a covenant written on the heart.

The *Catechism* offers some lovely paragraphs on this new covenant, but let me highlight just a few choice phrases. "The New Law or the Law of the Gospel is the perfection here on earth of the divine law, natural and revealed. It is the work of Christ and is expressed particularly in the Sermon on the Mount. It is also the work of the Holy Spirit and through him it becomes the interior law of charity" (1965). It's that last phrase that especially calls to mind Jeremiah's words. This new covenant written on the heart is the law of charity. This law is expressed in the twofold commandment to love God and neighbor, but it is not only an external "rule". As the *Catechism* says, it is the *interior* law of charity. It's the grace of Christ, his love within us.

Which is where the *Catechism* goes next: "The New Law is the *grace of the Holy Spirit* given to the faithful through faith in Christ. It works through charity; it uses the Sermon on the Mount to teach us what must be done and makes use of the sacraments to give us the grace to do it" (1966). This passage presents us the essentials of living out this new covenant written on the heart: grace, working through charity; following Christ's teaching, summed up in the Sermon on the Mount; and partaking of the sacraments, which contain and communicate the grace we need to follow Jesus and his teaching.

God knows that the divisions in the world are rife; he knows that the root cause of these divisions runs deep, as deep as the human heart, which is divided in itself. Even Saint Paul laments, "I do not do the good I want, but the evil I do not want is what I do" (Rom 7:19). And he explains, "If I do what I do not want, it is no longer I that do it, but sin that dwells within me. ... For I delight in the law of God, in my inmost self, but I see in my members another law at war ... the law of sin" (Rom 7:20, 22–23). God knows these wounds, our sins, and how deep they go. This is why he gives us the gift of a new covenant: written on the heart, the interior law of charity, the grace of the Holy Spirit poured into our hearts and transforming us from the inside out. Only in this way can the divisions we all experience be healed.

But it starts deep within each one of us. We can examine our consciences—and we should ... often! When we do that, the first step is usually to identify both our successes and our failures over the course of a day or part of a day. We give thanks for the former; we ask forgiveness for the latter. But because sin and division run so deep, after becoming aware of our sins, we should also explore our underlying motivations: what led me to this particular sin? What deeper struggle is going on within me? Did I speak a falsehood about myself or someone else out of envy? Or out of a desire for reputation or money or to impress someone? Did I take what wasn't mine because, out of pride, I thought it should be mine, or, out of greed, I wanted more or wanted the power it brings with it? This continuation of our examination of conscience takes a little more time, a little more reflection, and a little more effort. It isn't always easy. But we do it because God wants to send the roots of charity just as deeply down into our hearts. He wants that covenant to be written on every part of our hearts, so to speak. By looking to our deeper motivations, we allow the Holy Spirit to continue his work of purifying us so that the divisions within us can be healed … so that what is divided all around us can be united.

As we approach the final days of Advent, we might feel that burden of waiting, as God's Chosen People certainly did. Now is the time to shore up our hearts and efforts—to dig deep and, like God's wandering and divided people, to come face to face with the divisions within ourselves. That way, when Christ comes to us at Christmas, we'll welcome him with even greater joy and gratitude, knowing that he is the one who ushers in a new covenant, to heal and to bind up what is wounded, broken, and divided within us.

Questions for Reflection and Discussion

- Are there particular situations where you feel the divisions or tensions within your own heart most powerfully?

- Are there areas in your life where you notice the prompting of charity more frequently, more strongly?

Resolutions to Consider

- Examine your conscience tonight in a deeper way than usual, looking not only at your victories or failures but also the motivations behind each.

- Think of a relationship in your life that is troubled by division; commit to an action that will help to heal that division.

Build a Family Tradition

- With your family, read or tell in your own words Jeremiah's prophecy of a new covenant in Jeremiah 31.

- Draw attention to how unusual and hopeful the focus on unity is. Note the main point: God desires a new covenant for his people, not written in stone but on the heart.

- Hang up your Jesse Tree ornament. (Suggested image: a heart with writing on it)

- Discuss the following: *Does thinking about God's law being written on your heart feel like a burden, a joy, or maybe a little of both?*

Day 22

How to Be a Sheep

The Story of Salvation: Ezekiel 34:11–16

*"For thus says the Lord GOD: Behold, I, I myself will search for
my sheep, and will seek them out. As a shepherd seeks out his
flock when some of his sheep have been scattered abroad, so will
I seek out my sheep; and I will rescue them from all places where
they have been scattered on a day of clouds and thick darkness.
And I will bring them out from the peoples, and gather them
from the countries, and will bring them into their own land; and
I will feed them on the mountains of Israel, by the fountains,
and in all the inhabited places of the country. I will feed them
with good pasture, and upon the mountain heights of Israel shall
be their pasture; there they shall lie down in good grazing land,
and on fat pasture they shall feed on the mountains of Israel. I
myself will be the shepherd of my sheep, and I will make them
lie down, says the Lord GOD. I will seek the lost, and I will bring*

back the strayed, and I will bind up the crippled, and I will strengthen the weak, and the fat and the strong I will watch over; I will feed them in justice."

A Meditation for Today

On the mantel above our fireplace stands a statue of Christ the Good Shepherd. It's a beautiful one, a beloved wedding gift from years ago. It's also one of my favorite things to gaze at and meditate upon during prayer. The way Christ is depicted combines two biblical images. One is the Good Shepherd from John 10. The other is from Luke 15, the parable of the lost sheep, where a man leaves the ninety-nine to find the one that is lost, and when he finds it, "he lays it on his shoulders, rejoicing" (Lk 15:5). So, this statue has Jesus with a sheep over his shoulders. But one of the details that always strikes me is how the sheep lays over Jesus' shoulders. It almost melts into him, as though it has no strength left and must instead rely so completely on Jesus' strength that it becomes one with him. It combines and expresses a set of attributes that seem contradictory: being weak and vulnerable but also peaceful, joyful, and full of love for the shepherd and his shoulders.

This is what comes to mind when I hear today's prophecy in Ezekiel. The image of the shepherd is applied here on a larger scale. It refers to the Messiah seeking out the lost sheep of Israel, the divided and exiled tribes, and bringing them once again into the Promised Land and into unity. But as we look toward Christ's coming in Advent, we think also of how

Jesus applied this image to the one lost and helpless sheep—which is each one of us.

Both are true: Jesus comes to reunite all of Israel and to bring them, along with the Gentiles, into the kingdom of God. *And* he comes to seek and to save the lost, the sick, the sinner. His love is both intimately personal and powerfully social, even cosmic. But in either of these scenarios, what is striking is how much God emphasizes his own agency and action in this work of restoration: *I, I myself* will search for *my* sheep ... *I* will seek them ... *I* will rescue them ... *I* will bring them out ... *I* will feed them ... *I myself* will be their shepherd.

There's no doubt it can be very moving and consoling that God takes matters into his own hands and comes after us. But once he finds us and picks us up, so to speak, I think it can also challenge us in a certain way. Here's what I mean. In the moral life, we often think in terms of maturing and getting stronger. We even speak about the sacraments in this way, from baptism, to confirmation, to holy Eucharist, to marriage, priesthood, or the religious life. Through it all we grow into maturity, we make more and more choices for the good, we flex our spiritual muscles, we become *adults*. Which is just as it should be because Jesus says, "Unless you turn and become like adults, you will never enter the kingdom of heaven" (see Mt 18:3). And Saint John writes, "See what love the Father has given us, that we should be called adults of God" (see 1 Jn 3:1). No! Of course both of these passages speak about *children*, not adults.

Clearly this doesn't mean we should be child-*ish* or lack maturity. It means we grow to rely more and more on God. We have to learn, like the sheep that Jesus lays on his shoulders, to let ourselves be carried by our Lord. The maturity that the Christian strives for has less to do with learning to be increasingly active and more to do with learning to be increasingly receptive. This is true in ordinary, day-to-day life, where grace, the theological virtues, and especially the gifts of the Holy Spirit, guide and prompt us in our decisions and actions. It's God who gives us his grace and who ultimately moves us to the good.

This is also true, and even more so, in our prayer lives. The *Catechism* helps us to see and to remember that God is the protagonist in prayer, while we are receptive: referring to the story of the woman at the well (Jn 4), it says: "The wonder of prayer is revealed beside the well where we come seeking water: there, Christ comes to meet every human being. It is he who first seeks us and asks us for a drink. Jesus thirsts; his asking arises from the depths of God's desire for us. Whether we realize it or not, prayer is the encounter of God's thirst with ours. God thirsts that we may thirst for him" (2560). It is because God first thirsts for us that we thirst for him. It is because God, the Good Shepherd, seeks us that we seek him.

Nearing the end of Advent, our anticipation mounts as we look forward to Christ's birth. He enters into our world to enact in the most remarkable way God, God himself, seeking out the lost sheep of Israel. He takes matters into his own hands and comes after us. So what can we do? Well, we can receive that, we can give thanks for that, we can let ourselves be carried by the Lord. We acknowledge that in our Christian lives and in our prayer, so much depends on learning to be more receptive. But one great sign of growth—and something that contributes indirectly to growth—is learning to seek out and help those who are lost and unable to help themselves. It might not take us far afield to follow the scent of the sheep and to change that diaper. But it also *could* take us a little further away as we serve those in need, for example, bringing a meal to the sick or recovering. As we live the gospel more and more generously, our hearts are widened to receive more and more of God in prayer, to be found by him there, to encounter the Good Shepherd and simply to rest on his shoulders, to be carried by his strength, to be warmed by his love.

Questions for Reflection and Discussion

- How do you react to the idea of relying less on your own activity and more on God's? Do you find it comforting, empowering, frustrating, anxiety-inducing?

- Have you ever thought about prayer as a place where your efforts coincide with God's? Whose efforts do you tend to emphasize?

Resolutions to Consider

- Commit to being quieter and listening more in prayer.

- Remind yourself each morning this week that you need to rely more on God.

- When you feel down, frustrated, or lost, envision yourself as a sheep upon the Lord's shoulders and thank him for holding you close.

Build a Family Tradition

- With your family, read or tell in your own words the prophecy of the Lord seeking out his people in Ezekiel 34.

- Point out how God's action is center stage. Mention the main point: God will work to reunite his people and to draw us close to himself.

- Hang up your Jesse Tree ornament. (Suggested image: a sheep)

- Discuss the following: *How does Jesus protect us and guide us as the Good Shepherd?*

Day 23

A Covenant of Love

The Story of Salvation: Hosea 2:13–20

"And I will punish her for the feast days of the Ba'als
  when she burned incense to them
and decked herself with her ring and jewelry,
  and went after her lovers
  and forgot me, says the LORD.

"Therefore, behold, I will allure her,
  and bring her into the wilderness,
  and speak tenderly to her.
And there I will give her her vineyards,
  and make the Valley of A'chor a door of hope.
And there she shall answer as in the days of her youth,
  as at the time when she came out of the land of Egypt.

> "And in that day, says the LORD, you will call me 'My husband,'
> and no longer will you call me 'My Ba'al.' For I will remove the
> names of the Ba'als from her mouth, and they shall be mentioned
> by name no more. And I will make for you a covenant on that
> day with the beasts of the field, the birds of the air, and the creep-
> ing things of the ground; and I will abolish the bow, the sword,
> and war from the land; and I will make you lie down in safety.
> And I will espouse you for ever; I will espouse you in righteousness
> and in justice, in steadfast love, and in mercy. I will espouse you
> in faithfulness; and you shall know the LORD."

A Meditation for Today

Looking at these striking verses, two important themes come to mind:
covenant and wilderness.

First, the covenant. Here, God speaks of forging another covenant, a
new covenant, with his people. We've heard this before in a prophecy
of Jeremiah. You remember it: "Behold, the days are coming ... when
I will make a new covenant with the house of Israel and the house of
Judah ... I will put my law within them, and I will write it upon their
hearts" (Jer 31:31–33). Jeremiah speaks of a new covenant written on
the heart. Hosea also presents a covenant of the heart, but it has a different character.

In Jeremiah, the new covenant is spoken of in legal terms—a new
law—so when God says there, "I will be their God, and they shall be my
people" (Jer 31:33), it sounds like the relation between ruler and ruled.

And that's perfectly apt: God is God, the ruler of the universe, and we are to be obedient to him for our own good. In Hosea, the resonance is very different. The context is *nuptial*: "I will espouse you for ever," says God. So, when God speaks in this way—or when he says, "I will allure her ... I will speak tenderly to her"—it sounds like the relation between a lover and his beloved.

The *Catechism* highlights how this imagery is at the heart of God's plan of salvation: "The nuptial covenant between God and his people Israel had prepared the way for the new and everlasting covenant in which the Son of God, by becoming incarnate and giving his life, has united to himself in a certain way all mankind saved by him, thus preparing for 'the wedding-feast of the Lamb'" (1612).

Taking in this spousal imagery helps to round out the picture for us of what God's covenant with his people, with us, is like. It's a legal reality: it's a law, and we are invited and expected to follow it. It has a familial dimension as well, since kinship bonds can be established through a covenant, and in this covenant, we are invited to be children of God. And it's a gift and bond of love. God loves his people—he loves us tremendously—and he invites us to respond to that love.

Images of all three of these realities run through the Old Testament, as we've already seen in the story of Abraham, where the familial dimension clearly emerges. We've also seen it in Exodus and Jeremiah, where the legal dimension stands at the forefront. And now we've seen it in Hosea, where the language of love shines forth, as it also does in the love poetry of the Song of Songs.

In the New Testament, these same dimensions can be found. What we wait for during Advent is the coming of the New Moses, the giver of the New Law ... and the coming of God's Son, who will make us his brothers and sisters, who can call upon God as "our Father" ... and the coming of the long-awaited Bridegroom, who will lay down his life and give himself entirely to us in love. Christ embodies all three of these dimensions in himself, and one of the fruits of our Jesse Tree reflections is that we can appreciate each of these dimensions even more at Christmas because we've encountered and lived them this Advent.

Now, the second theme: the wilderness, or the desert. What is the desert? There are a lot of things we could say about the desert, but as Hosea makes clear, the desert is ultimately a place of wooing: "Behold, I will allure her, and bring her into the wilderness, and speak tenderly to her" (Hos 2:14). God leads his people into the wilderness in order to draw them close to him. And he does the same with us.

What is it about the wilderness that makes it a place of being wooed by God and drawing close to him? First of all, it's a place of need. With scarce resources, our needs and fragility are hard to overlook. We realize quickly how much we rely on God, something we often forget when we're in places of abundance and comfort. Second, the wilderness is a place of simplicity. There's quiet, there's sand or dirt, there's minimal vegetation, and not much else. We are alone with ourselves and, we come to find out, alone with God. In the desert, we can hear God's voice better because there's less noise, less distraction, less comfort.

When we keep this in mind—that the wilderness is a place of self-knowledge, a place to acknowledge our needs, and a place to hear God's voice—then the desert turns out to be a place of abundance. Not the type of abundance we usually think of, where we have many things, but rather the type of abundance where we have only one thing, but it's the greatest thing, the one thing necessary, the better part. In the desert, we have God.

The deserts in our lives are not usually literal deserts. More likely, they are challenges or times of loneliness or suffering. Prayer involves deserts, too, where we suffer from not praying, or we pray, but we feel distant from God in prayer or as though our hearts aren't warmed by his presence in prayer as they once were. All of these kinds of deserts are very normal in the Christian life, and they are meant to be times of richness and depth—when we embrace them and avoid their temptations. The temptation is often to feel that God is far, that we are alone, or that it's too uncomfortable. Then we flee the desert. But if we can embrace it and persevere, especially in prayer, then the Lord will come to meet us, to woo us, and to speak to us as his beloved.

As we prepare our hearts for Christ's coming, we remember that at the beginning of his public ministry, Jesus was also drawn to the desert. There he faced temptation, persevered, and emerged ready for a new phase of his life. Like him, we, too, must go through the wilderness, but like him, we also are not alone. We can rely on our heavenly Father for companionship, solace, strength, and love when he leads us into the desert to woo our hearts once again.

Questions for Reflection and Discussion

- Think about the deserts in your own life. What kinds of situations are they? What sufferings and what fruits have you found there?

- If the desert is a place of encounter, how can we insert more desert-like spaces in our lives?

Resolutions to Consider

- Identify one situation in your life right now that is desert-like and ask God to manifest himself to you in it.

- Commit to reading the Song of Songs and seeing it as a dialogue of love between Christ and your soul.

- Remind your friends or your family of how much God loves us.

Build a Family Tradition

- With your family, read or tell in your own words the beautiful prophecy in Hosea 2.

- Highlight the spousal imagery used. Note the main point: God loves his people and also us.

- Hang up your Jesse Tree ornament. (Suggested image: wedding rings)

- Discuss the following: *What do betrothal and marriage teach us about God's love for us?*

Day 24

Hidden with Christ

The Story of Salvation: Luke 1:26–38

*In the sixth month the angel Gabriel was sent from God to a city
of Galilee named Nazareth, to a virgin betrothed to a man whose
name was Joseph, of the house of David; and the virgin's name
was Mary. And he came to her and said, "Hail, full of grace,
the Lord is with you!" But she was greatly troubled at the saying,
and considered in her mind what sort of greeting this might be.
And the angel said to her, "Do not be afraid, Mary, for you have
found favor with God. And behold, you will conceive in your
womb and bear a son, and you shall call his name Jesus.*

> *He will be great and will be called the Son of the Most High;
> and the Lord God will give to him the throne of his father David,
> and he will reign over the house of Jacob for ever;
> and of his kingdom there will be no end."*

And Mary said to the angel, "How will this be, since I have no husband?" And the angel said to her,

> *"The Holy Spirit will come upon you,*
> *and the power of the Most High will overshadow you;*
> *therefore the child to be born will be called holy,*
> *the Son of God.*

And behold, your relative Elizabeth in her old age has also conceived a son; and this is the sixth month with her who was called barren. For with God nothing will be impossible." And Mary said, "Behold, I am the handmaid of the Lord; let it be to me according to your word." And the angel departed from her.

A Meditation for Today

Right at the beginning of its teaching on Mary, the *Catechism* makes this claim: "What the Catholic faith believes about Mary is based on what it believes about Christ, and what it teaches about Mary illumines in turn its faith in Christ" (487). Then, the *Catechism* unpacks the phrase in the Creed, "born of the Virgin Mary." Even this phrase targets Christ first: *he* is the one who enters the world through Mary.

Our reading today bears out this same logic. We don't learn very much about Mary in a direct way, who she is, what she's like. Instead, the account takes a different angle in its opening phrases.

"The angel Gabriel"—it begins with an angelic messenger—"was sent from God"—now we get the main protagonist, the one who's directing things—"to a city of Galilee named Nazareth"—this establishes some historical and geographical roots, but also some roots in salvation history—"to a virgin betrothed to a man whose name was Joseph"— Joseph is actually the first human name mentioned—"of the house of David." The weight of the sentence lands at the end, emphasizing the Davidic line, something we've seen before. And then, almost like an afterthought (though I think one filled with tender affection): "and the virgin's name was Mary."

So, what do we learn about Mary in these lines and the dialogue that follows? At the most fundamental level, we learn that her identity and her life are radically defined by an intervention and a call from God. Remarkable things can indeed be said of her: she's "full of grace", immaculately conceived; she is to be both virgin and mother; she is perfectly docile and receptive to the Lord's will. But all of these things are inseparable from—and even unintelligible apart from—the special mission and role to which God has called her. What we know of Mary is radically determined by her son, Jesus, and her unique relation to him. Just as the *Catechism* says, what we believe about Mary is based on what we believe about Christ.

Remember our discussion of Abram as a man fundamentally defined by an unexpected call and the future it opens before him? What we know of Abram, later Abraham, is radically determined *by* that call and *because* of that call. Without God's surprising invitation and Abraham's response of faith, we would probably know nothing about him.

Mary's story runs in parallel to Abraham's, and, like Abraham's, her life is defined and determined by her astonishing faith in Christ, in the promise of his birth and mission, and in her magnificent role in both. As we await Christ's coming at Christmas, we can imagine Mary's anticipation for the birth of this child. Not only is he the Son of God and *her* son, but he is the one who so completely shapes her life, gives it its meaning, and causes it to be remembered and honored throughout history. It is entirely because of him that Mary says, "all generations will call me blessed" (Lk 1:48).

All of this reminds me of a lovely little expression that Saint Paul uses: "For you have died, and your life is hidden with Christ in God" (Col 3:3). He's reminding early Christians that to be Christian is to have died with Christ, through faith and baptism, in order to rise again with him to new life. And the life we are called to live is "hidden in Christ"—it takes on the shape of Christ's life as we grow closer to him, are conformed to him, and imitate him more and more. Mary's life is the perfect example of being "hidden in Christ". She is so like her son that who she is and how we know her are based entirely on him. Her identity is truly "hidden in Christ" and were it not for him, we'd know nothing of her.

This is true of Mary in a unique way, but our lives, too, are meant to be "hidden in Christ". When we consider other saints of the Church, very few of them would have been remembered by history were it not for their relation to Christ, their devotion to him, and their sanctity. In this, they show us that to live our lives "hidden in Christ" means that the recognition we hope most to receive is that of being a Christian, a friend and a disciple of Christ.

What about you? If you were to enter into the pages of history, what story would you most hope to have told of you? The story of *your* accomplishments or of a life radically defined by *Christ's* call, a life close to Christ, so "hidden in Christ" as to be unintelligible apart from him?

Mary, our Lady, is someone who had God at the center of all she did. From her, we can learn how to make ourselves "unknown" and "unknowable" apart from Christ by putting him first so that our lives are radically determined by him and by our love for him.

What is one thing you could do today to put Christ first in your life, to make him your first love? If we can do that, day after day, then the next line that Saint Paul writes in Colossians 3 will also be true of us: "When Christ who is your life appears, then you also will appear with him in glory." When our lives are hidden in Christ, like Mary's, then we will one day share in his glory.

Questions for Reflection and Discussion

- Think about the people in your life, maybe your coworkers, your inner circle friends, your spouse, your children. If they were to write an account of you and your life, would God be at the center? Would *his* work—for you, in you, through you—be at the center?

- What worries do you have about putting Christ first in a way that makes your life "hidden in Christ"?

Resolutions to Consider

- Pray Mary's Magnificat (Lk 1:46–55) each day this week.

- Identify one area in your life where you'd rather stand out than be "hidden in Christ". Commit to some action that will exercise humility in this area.

- Pray a rosary and meditate on Mary's hiddenness in Christ.

Build a Family Tradition

- With your family, read or tell in your own words the story of the Annunciation in Luke 1.

- Point out how Mary is both honored by the angel and humble before God. Note the main point: Mary says yes to God's plan, placing her life completely in God's service.

- Hang up your Jesse Tree ornament. (Suggested image: Mary)

- Discuss the following: *What are some lessons we can learn from Mary?*

Day 25

The Adventure

The Story of Salvation: Matthew 1:1–6, 12–16, 18–24

The book of the genealogy of Jesus Christ, the son of David, the son of Abraham. Abraham begot Isaac, Isaac begot Jacob, Jacob begot Judah and his brothers, Judah begot Perez and Zerah by Tamar, Perez begot Hezron, Hezron begot Aram, Aram begot Aminadab, Aminadab begot Nahshon, Nahshon begot Salmon, Salmon begot Boaz by Rahab, Boaz begot Obed by Ruth, Obed begot Jesse, and Jesse begot David the king.

David begot Solomon by the wife of Uriah ...

After the Babylonian exile, Jechoniah begot Shealtiel, Shealtiel begot Zerubbabel, Zerubbabel begot Abiud, Abiud begot Eliakim, Eliakim begot Azor, Azor begot Zadok, Zadok begot Achim, Achim begot Eliud, Eliud begot Eleazar, Eleazar begot Matthan, Matthan begot Jacob, and Jacob begot Joseph the husband of Mary, of whom Jesus was born, who is called the Christ. . . .

Now the birth of Jesus Christ took place in this way. When his mother Mary had been betrothed to Joseph, before they came together, she was found to be with child of the Holy Spirit. And Joseph her husband, being a righteous man and unwilling to expose her to shame, decided to divorce her secretly. But while he was considered these things, behold, an angel of the Lord appeared to him in a dream, saying, "Joseph, son of David, do not fear to take Mary your wife, for the child conceived in her is of the Holy Spirit. She will bear a son, and you shall call his name Jesus, for he will save his people from their sins." Now all so that what was spoken by the Lord through the prophet might be fulfilled,

> *"Behold, the virgin shall be with child*
> *and bear a son, and they shall*
> *call his name Emmanuel,"*

which means, "God with us." When Joseph rose from sleep, he did as the angel of the Lord commanded him.

A Meditation for Today

I have a confession to make. When I was a child, I used to dread this reading coming up at Mass. It seemed to be just a list of names that went on and on. "Will it never end?!" I thought to myself.

Not my finest moment, I admit. Now that I'm older, I do realize that it isn't just a list of names, but sometimes—especially when I'm wrangling a toddler in the pew—I do still find myself thinking, "It's going on and on … "

But actually, I'm okay with that. In a way, the opening of Saint Matthew's Gospel gives us just a little taste of the long and arduous waiting of God's Chosen People for the coming of the Messiah.

It does this not only by perhaps taxing our patience but also by filling our minds and imaginations with characters and scenes from Jesus' storied genealogy … which are now even more familiar to us! The extraordinary greatness of Abraham, Moses, and David. The ordinary heroism of Ruth or Boaz. The temptation and struggles of Cain or Jacob. The endurance and mercy of Joseph. And so on.

All of this leads up to and lives on in Saint Joseph—it's his story. Because of him, it becomes Jesus' story. And, as we've seen, it's our story, too. But let's dwell for a moment on Joseph.

When Saint Matthew's genealogy reaches Joseph, there's a shift in the pattern because, of course, Joseph's role is different: "Joseph, the husband of Mary, of whom Jesus was born." But, despite this difference, Joseph is very much in the line of the great patriarchs of the Old Testament. God intervenes dramatically in his life and sets him on a path that is new and entirely unexpected. He sends an angel—more than once!—to prepare him to accept Mary as his wife and, with that, to accept his role as the earthly father of Jesus, the Son of God.

This was, in a sense, the beginning of Joseph's adventure, preparing for Christ's birth. Remember how we said on day 7 that adventure suggests something that comes toward us in a way unforeseen? This is exactly what happened to Joseph, and it coincides with the first Advent: awaiting the birth of Christ in an especially personal and intimate way. Joseph is a man of adventure. There's the adventure that begins with obeying God, taking Mary as his wife, and accepting his role in this great mystery. Then, they have to set off for Bethlehem to fulfill the census requirements. Which is also quite an adventure, as anyone who's traveled with a significantly pregnant wife knows! Then, there are all the unknowns and challenges Joseph has to deal with in Bethlehem leading up to Christ's birth. Even after his birth, there's the flight to Egypt, when—we notice again—there is a divine intervention, an unexpected challenge, and the obedience that leads to ... adventure.

For Joseph, this time of waiting, of expectation, of anticipation was truly an adventure, the beginning of that larger adventure of being the earthly father of God's incarnate Son.

Joseph is a model of allowing God's will to break in upon our lives, which are often too comfortable and neat, and to redirect us toward the true adventure of living life alongside Christ. He's a model of preparing ourselves for Christ's coming, not only through prayer and reflection but also through action ... acting well, working with excellence, taking care of things, being obedient to God's will, loving well. In the Gospels, Joseph is not a man of many words. But he is a man of *action*. He is an exemplar of that virtue we call prudence. As the *Catechism* reminds us, prudence shouldn't be confused with timidity or fear or being overly calculating. Instead, it "disposes practical reason to discern our true good in every circumstance and to choose the right means of achieving it" (1806). Prudence discerns and it chooses; it deliberates and it acts. It is decisive. Joseph was all of these things *to a tee*. His adventure demanded it of him. And so he models the *Catechism*'s summary here: that "prudence is 'right reason in action.'" Following Saint Joseph, in Advent, we are to pray, we are to reflect, *and* we are to take action!

"Now you tell me! On the last day!" Well, if you've been following along, you have taken action in various ways! And if not, it's not too late! Take action now (see the resolutions below).

But even more important is to bear in mind that the adventure of Advent doesn't stop at Christmas—it continues long after Christ's birth, for the whole of our lives. All the stories and figures we've seen and reflected on in these Jesse Tree reflections continue in our own lives. Because *this is our story*. The long and winding story of salvation that Joseph embodies continues in our lives. The Jesse Tree is our family tree, and in it, we've found not only tales of old but the story of our own longings and hopes, our own failings and faithlessness, our own victories and virtues. This tree is not perfectly straight; it's not perfectly purebred. But, God who writes straight with crooked lines, who works all things for good, brings it to perfection in Christ and in the marvelous and abundant fruit it can bear in each of our lives. So, take heart and take action. The adventure of Advent nears its end, but the adventure of Christ's life and our life "hidden in him"—*that* is just beginning.

Questions for Reflection and Discussion

- What do you think about Saint Joseph's role in salvation history?

- What can Saint Joseph teach you about being a disciple of Christ?

Resolutions to Consider

- Set aside 20 or 30 minutes today to pray with the genealogy, reflecting on the familiar characters and their stories.

- Buy or make something that prepares your home and your heart for Christ's coming.

- Make one significant sacrifice today out of love, like Saint Joseph sacrificing so much to care for Mary and to help bring Christ into the world.

Build a Family Tradition

- With your family, read or tell in your own words the genealogy of Jesus Christ in Matthew 1.

- Appreciate how familiar some of the names are now after going through these Jesse Tree reflections. Note the main point: Christ comes into the world through the faithfulness of Saint Joseph and Mary.

- Hang up your Jesse Tree ornament. (Suggested image: Nativity scene or crib)

- Discuss the following: *What do you think Saint Joseph was like as a father?*

Conclusion

Merry Christmas!

"Glory to God in the highest, and on earth peace among men with whom he is pleased!" (Luke 2:14)

Thank you so very much for joining me on this Advent journey of rediscovering the Jesse Tree and our roots in it. It's *our* family tree and it's meant to bear fruit in our lives, especially by making us ready to welcome Christ in the Christmas mystery. As our thoughts and prayers turn toward the holy child in the manger, my hope is that you've felt yourself more deeply rooted this Advent and that tapping into these roots has already begun to bear good fruit in your life.

May the Lord grant you an abundant harvest and a most joyful celebration of Christmas!